MERCE CUNNINGHAM

Select Other Works by Richard Kostelanetz

Books Authored

The Theatre of Mixed Means (1968)
Master Minds (1969)
Visual Language (1970)
In the Beginning (1971)
The End of Intelligent Writing (1974)
Openings & Closings (1975)
Portraits from Memory (1975)
Constructs (1975)
One Night Stood (1977)
Wordsand (1978)
Twenties in the Sixties (1979)
And So Forth (1979)
Metamorphosis in the Arts (1980)
The Old Poetries and the New (1981)
American Imaginations (1983)
The Old Fictions and the New (1987)
Conversing with Cage (1988)
On Innovative Music(ian)s (1989)
The New Poetries and Some Old (1991)
Politics in the African-American Novel
   (1991)
Solos, Duets, Trios, & Choruses (1991)
On Innovative Art(ist)s (1992)
Wordworks: Poems Selected & New
   (1993)
A Dictionary of the Avant-Garde (1993)
Minimal Fictions (1994)
Fillmore East: Recollections of Rock
   Theater (1995)
An ABC of Contemporary Reading
   (1995)
One Million Words of Booknotes (1995)
Radio Writing (1995)
Crimes of Culture (1996)
John Cage (Ex)plain(ed) (1996)

Books Edited

On Contemporary Literature (1964, 1969)
Twelve from the Sixties (1967)
The Young American Writers (1967)
Possibilities of Poetry (1970)
Imaged Words & Worded Images (1970)
Moholy-Nagy (1970, 1991)
John Cage (1970, 1991)
Seeing Through Shuck (1972)
Breakthrough Fictioneers (1973)
The Edge of Adaptation (1973)
Essaying Essays (1975)
Language & Structure (1975)
Younger Critics in North America (1976)
Esthetics Contemporary (1978, 1989)
Assembling Assembling (1978)
Visual Literature Criticism (1979)
Text-Sound Texts (1980)
The Yale Gertrude Stein (1980)
Aural Literature Criticism (1981)
The Literature of SoHo (1981)
American Writing Today (1981, 1991)
The Avant-Garde Tradition in
   Literature (1982)
Gertrude Stein Advanced (1989)
The B. B. King Companion (1997)
The Frank Zappa Companion (1997)
Writings on Glass (1997)

Books Co-authored & Edited

The New American Arts (1965)

Books Co-compiled & Introduced

Assembling (Twelve vols., 1970–1981)

MERCE CUNNINGHAM

Dancing in Space and Time

EDITED BY RICHARD KOSTELANETZ

Essays 1944–1992 by Jack Anderson, John Cage, Remy Charlip, Arlene Croce, Merce Cunningham, Nancy Dalva, Don Daniels, Edwin Denby, Barbara Frost, Jill Johnston, Kenneth King, Alastair Macaulay, Don McDonagh, Wilfrid Mellers, Frank O'Hara, Sybil Shearer, Marcia B. Siegel, Stephen Smoliar, Calvin Tomkins, David Vaughan, James Waring, and the Editor; Symposia including Carolyn Brown, Earle Brown, Remy Charlip, Douglas Dunn, Viola Farber, Steve Paxton, Valda Setterfield, Marianne Preger Simon, Gus Solomons jr, and David Vaughan.

DA CAPO PRESS • NEW YORK

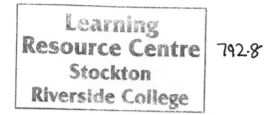
Library of Congress Cataloging-in-Publication Data

Merce Cunningham: dancing in space and time / edited by Richard Kostelanetz: essays 1944–1992 by Jack Anderson ... [et al.].—1st Da Capo Press ed.

    p.   cm.

  Originally published: Chicago: Chicago Review Press: Distributed by Independent Publishers Group, c1992.

  Includes bibliographical references (p.) and index.

  ISBN 0-306-80877-3 (pbk.)

  1. Cunningham, Merce. 2. Dancers—United States—Biography. 3. Choreographers—United States—Biography. 4. Modern dance—United States—History. I. Kostelanetz, Richard. II. Anderson, Jack, 1935– .

[GV1785.C85M48 1998]

792.8′028′092—dc21

[B]

98-6776
CIP

First Da Capo Press edition 1998

This Da Capo Press paperback edition of *Merce Cunningham* is an unabridged republication of the edition first published in Chicago in 1992, with three minor textual emendations. It is reprinted by arrangement with the editor.

Published by Da Capo Press, Inc.
A Subsidiary of Plenum Publishing Corporation
233 Spring Street, New York, N.Y. 10013

ACKNOWLEDGMENTS

Jack Anderson, "Dances About Everything and Dances About Some Things." In *Choreography Observed*. Iowa City, IA: U. of Iowa Press, 1987. Copyright © 1975, 1987 by Jack Anderson.

Carolyn Brown, contributions to a symposium in *Ballet Review* (1987), by permission of the author.

Earle Brown, contributions to a symposium in *Ballet Review* (1985), by permission of the author.

John Cage, "Grace and Clarity." In *Silence*. Middletown, CT: Wesleyan U. Press, 1961. By permission of the publisher and the University Press of New England. Copyright © 1961 by John Cage.

Remy Charlip, "Composing by Chance." *Dance Magazine* (January 1954); contributions to a symposium in *Ballet Review* (1985), by permission of the author. Copyright © 1954/1992, 1985 by Remy Charlip.

Arlene Croce, "The Mercists." *The New Yorker* (3 April 1978), by permission of the author. Copyright © 1978 by Arlene Croce.

Merce Cunningham, "Space, Time and Dance." *Trans/Formation* I/3 (1952); "A Collaborative Process Between Music and Dance." *Tri-Quarterly* 54 (1982); reprinted by permission of the author. Copyright © 1952, 1982 by Merce Cunningham. "Diary of a Cunningham Dance." *The New York Times* (15 March 1981), copyright © 1981 by the New York Times Company, reprinted by permission of *The New York Times* and Merce Cunningham.

Nancy Dalva, "The Way of Merce." *Dance Ink* III/1 (Spring 1992). By permission of the author. Copyright © 1992 by Nancy Dalva.

Don Daniels, "Cunningham in Time," excerpted from "Boutique Items and Risky Business." *Ballet Review* XIII/2 (Summer 1985), by permission of the author. Copyright © 1985 by Don Daniels.

Edwin Denby, reviews reprinted from the *New York Herald Tribune* by permission of Rudy Burkhardt for the Estate of Edwin Denby.

Douglas Dunn, contributions to a symposium in *Ballet Review* (1987), by permission of the author.

Viola Farber, contributions to a symposium in *Ballet Review* (1987), by permission of the author.

Barbara Frost, "Merce Cunningham." *Vassar Brew* (1948), reprinted from the public domain.

Jill Johnston, reviews from *The Village Voice*, reprinted by permission of the author.

Kenneth King, "Space Dance and the Galactic Matrix," previously unpublished, by permission of the author. Copyright © 1991 by Kenneth King. Portions appeared in *Chicago Review* (1992).

Richard Kostelanetz, excerpt from "Artists' Self-Books." *Ballet Review* III/2 (1969), reprinted in *Twenties in the Sixties* (Brooklyn, NY: Assembling; Westport, CT: Greenwood Press, 1979), by permission of the author. Copyright © 1969, 1979 by Richard Kostelanetz. "Twenty Years of Merce Cunningham's Dance," revised from *Dance Magazine* (1982), by permission of the author. Copyright © 1982, 1992 by Richard Kostelanetz.

Alastair Macaulay, "The Merce Experience." *The New Yorker* (4 April 1988), by permission of the publisher. Copyright © 1988 by Alastair Macaulay.

Don McDonagh, "Merce Cunningham." In *Don McDonagh's Complete Guide to Modern Dance*. NY: Doubleday and Company, 1977, by permission of the author. Copyright © 1977 by Don McDonagh.

Wilfrid Mellers, "Tranquillity." *The New Statesman* (31 July 1964), by permission of the publisher.

Frank O'Hara. "Cunningham, Here and Now." *The Village Voice* (4 December 1957), reprinted from the public domain.

Steve Paxton, contributions to a symposium in *Ballet Review* (1987), by permission of the author.

Valda Setterfield, contributions to a symposium in *Ballet Review* (1987), by permission of the author.

Sybil Shearer, "Dance in Review." *Dance News* (March 1949), by permission of the author.

Marcia B. Siegel. "Come in, Earth. Are You There?" In *At the Vanishing Point* (NY: Saturday Review Press/E.P. Dutton, 1972), by permission of the author. Copyright © 1972 by Marcia B. Siegel.

Marianne Preger Simon, contributions to symposia in *Ballet Review* (1985, 1987), by permission of the author.

Stephen Smoliar, "Merce Cunningham in Brooklyn." *Ballet Review* III/3 (1970), by permission of the author. Copyright © 1970 by Stephen Smoliar.

Gus Solomons jr, contributions to a symposium in *Ballet Review* (1987), by permission of the author.

Calvin Tomkins, text for an exhibition by Merce Cunningham (Multiples, 1974), by permission of the author.

David Vaughan, "Merce Cunningham's *Walkaround Time*." In *Art and Dance* (Boston: Institute of Contemporary Art, 1982); "Retrospect and Prospect." *Performing Arts Journal* (Winter 1979); "Locale: The Collaboration of Merce Cunningham and Charles Atlas." *Millennium Film Journal* 10/11 (Fall–Winter 1981/82); contributions to symposia in *Ballet Review* (1985, 1987); all by permission of the author. Copyright © 1982, 1979, 1981, 1985, 1987 by David Vaughan.

James Waring, "Merce Cunningham: Maker of Dances." *The Village Voice* (2 January 1957), by permission of David Vaughan for the Estate of James Waring.

Every effort has been made to identify the sources of original publication of these essays and make full acknowledgment of their use. If any error or omission has occurred, it will be corrected in future editions, provided that appropriate notification is submitted in writing to the publisher or editor.

CONTENTS

extended critical considerations similar to those found in the best American literary journals—criticism written by experienced observers unconstrained by editorial concessions to audience and length, among other vulgarities. The people gathered in her parlor thought that dance criticism should be more ambitious, initially more extended and more serious, than that found in newspaper reviews. Whenever Denby spoke in his soft voice, the others would hush, so palpable was his authority. It seems apparent now that I was witnessing the beginnings of the more serious American dance criticism represented here, so it is scarcely surprising to find now that more contributions to this book come from *Ballet Review* than anywhere else. Except for historic documents originally published prior to 1965 (at the beginning of Cunningham's regular New York seasons), this book contains criticism, not reviews; the two are not the same.

I am grateful to Jill Johnston who insisted three decades ago that I see Cunningham's work, to Arlene Croce for founding *Ballet Review*, to David Vaughan for guiding me through the clippings he has collected as the Cunningham Company's veteran archivist and for sharing his bibliography of Cunningham criticism and chronology of Cunningham's choreography, to Anne Del Castillo for copyediting the manuscript and editorial advice, to Andrew Benker and Nicole Hinrichs for proofreading assistance, and finally to the contributors for granting me permission to reprint their materials.

The biggest problem for me has been, in truth, determining in what order the essays should appear. I tried various thematic schemes, in part to avoid redundancy, only to discover that because certain assumptions of Cunningham's dance were so unique to him critics would "discover" them over and over again. In the end, I resorted to a mostly chronological order that has the virtues (over, say, alphabetical order by contributors' names) of historical truth.

This book would have been dedicated to its subject, had he not already received another book of mine, *American Imaginations* (1985); it might have been dedicated to his longtime coconspirator, John Cage, had he too not received yet another book of mine, *Recyclings* (1984). And so it goes to Kenneth King, whose inspired essay prompted the vision of this anthology, though he insists, as he tells me, "It's all for Merce." For the past quarter century now, King has also been not only an adventurous choreographer but a loyal friend. Thanks, pal.

Richard Kostelanetz
New York
14 May 1991

Don McDonagh

MERCE CUNNINGHAM (1973)

Merce Cunningham was among the first to challenge the conventions of the founding generation of modern dance. His own career started on the West Coast. He was born in Centralia, Washington in 1919, and showed an early interest in dance instruction which was centered on popular forms, including tap, a style for which he retained a great fondness. At Cornish School of Fine and Applied Arts in Seattle, he continued his studies and became exposed to the musical ideas of John Cage, who was on its faculty in the late thirties. One summer, he attended the dance session at Mills College in Oakland, and danced in Lester Horton's *Conquest*. The following year, in 1939, the faculty of the Bennington College Summer School of the Dance, including Martha Graham, was resident at Mills College, and Cunningham was invited to join the Graham company in New York for the fall season. He was the second man to join her company.

He remained with the company until the mid-forties and created many roles, including the Revivalist in *Appalachian Spring*, the Acrobat in *Every Soul Is a Circus*, the Christ figure in *El Penitente*, and a sprightly solo "March" in *Letter to the World*. It was in this last role that great use was made of his nimble and high jump. He began to experiment with his own choreography at Bennington College, where he cochoreographed three works with Jean Erdman, a fellow member of the Graham company. He subsequently created solos for himself and formed an artistic alliance with John Cage as his musical director that persists to this day.

He formed his own company after leaving the Graham company and his work was increasingly marked by its new approach, which was not dependent on the accepted need for story, character, and dramatic mood. He was

1

develops forward toward the audience. Usually Cunningham allows his dances to transpire over the entire surface of the dance space, but in this one he chooses not to. The music has a menacing drone.

A man enters a totally deserted area and performs a short, cautious solo as if seeing strange territory for the first time. Suddenly he is joined by a woman, then three others; all are costumed in industrial-weight, transparent plastic subtly tinted blue, pink, green, and yellow. The others leave and he partners the first woman. They separate and he goes to the rear of the stage, where two small geodesic lights sit on a length of cloth. He lights the smaller of the two and rubs his shin reflectively as if meditating about an old hurt.

He kneels and slowly draws the cloth toward him. The others dance farther down the stage closer to the audience. He lights the second lamp. He stands and makes crisscross motions with his hands as if to ward off something, almost like a man brushing away annoying gnats or trying to get rid of troublesome thoughts. He is soberly clad in black, and the other men and women are in colored costumes. His second solo finds him still alone and isolated. The men and women change partners and carry through a rather cool series of duets like mating automatons. The man in black dances alone again, and, while the others involve themselves with one another, he tends the two lamps. The women drop one by one and are carried off by the men. When they have all left, the man in black walks forward to look around him at the deserted area. He returns to his solitary life, and this time he half slips into a plastic bag and wriggles, thrashing, along the floor. It is not clear whether he wants to be wholly in it or free from it, but the curtain descends as he is still thrashing.

The dance has a futuristic look in its see-through plastic costuming and geodesic lights and makes one feel very lonely and abandoned. The man tending his lights seems intent upon preserving something in the midst of this alien atmosphere, but, at the end, even he is driven to some display of emotional desperation as the last of the coolly distant inhabitants has left. He is not of like temperament and yet they both dwell in the same place virtually side by side, separated by an invisible wall of exclusion.

RainForest

Choreography by Merce Cunningham. Music by David Tudor. Scenery and costumes by Andy Warhol. First performed at the Upton Auditorium, Buffalo, NY, March 9, 1968, by Merce Cunningham, Carolyn Brown, Barbara Lloyd, Albert Reid, Sandra Neels, and Gus Solomons jr.

There is no rain to be seen or heard in the piece, and the "forest" is a cluster of inflated pillow shapes, but there is a strong feeling of a jungle setting in the choreography. Some of the silver pillows are filled with helium so that they float in the air above the dancers, and others are just tossed casually on the stage, to be moved by the breeze of the dancers passing. They provide a changing and playful backdrop to the somewhat animalistic dance. Just before the first performance, the designer Jasper Johns went around from dancer to dancer cutting little holes in the costumes so that the dancers would appear to be somewhat ragged in contrast to the smooth, shiny pillows.

Three figures are seen standing as the light slowly brightens. A man and a woman are close together and another man stands some distance away. All weave their arms and swirl in place. It appears as if they are stretching, suggesting the first movements of the day. The man and the woman now start to snake around one another; the movement is young, strong, almost rough. The first man leaves, and the one in the background moves forward to dance with the woman, after which they lie together.

A third man enters and together he and the other man push the lying woman to the edge of the stage. The man most recently arrived does a fast and assertive solo which attracts the woman, and they go off together. The second man stands and a second woman dashes on briskly and engages in an athletic romp with him, after which they go off together.

A third woman begins a proud, vital solo that attracts the attention of the first man who has returned. He joins her and creates the impression of a warrior, during which she leaves and he follows, to leave the stage bare of people but full of the slightly rocking and swaying pillows, serene as ever.

The dance is like a representation of life in a primitive society where relationships are simple and somewhat brutal. The suggestions of rooting and cavorting that are in the piece contrast wonderfully with the almost antiseptic decor, suggesting cave men in a computer era.

Changing Steps

Choreography by Merce Cunningham. Music by David Behrman, John Cage, Gordon Mumma, and David Tudor. Costumes by Charles Atlas. First performed as part of Event #65, Brooklyn Academy of Music, March 22, 1973, by Douglas Dunn, Meg Harper, Susana Hayman-Chaffey, Chris Komar, Robert Kovich, Barbara Lias, Brynar Mehl, Sandra Neels, Valda Setterfield, Julie Roess-Smith.

This exceptionally fine dance is a rarity in that it does not have a part for the choreographer himself. Ordinarily one expects to see him in each work, but this one was created for the members of his company and represents a beautiful and lean demonstration of Cunningham's style of movement as designed for others' talents, not just his own.

A man enters and performs a slow sequence of Adonis-like poses that are classically clean, and leaves after a few thrusts and leaps. A woman lyrically bends forward and backward, dancing lightly on the balls of her feet. A second woman dances a solo, entering the spot just vacated by the other. She turns the proscenium from end to end and from top to bottom. For nearly the entire piece the scene is bathed in hazy light whose overall murkiness is reminiscent of *Winterbranch*. (But whereas the earlier work is black and strident, *Inlets* is fair and mellow.) The music is a John Cage composition that sounds electronic but is actually the amplified sound of water jostled in large conch shells. (Why do amplified natural noises sound more like other amplified sound than anything heard in nature?) The crowning touch of the Morris Graves decor is a silver medallion, several feet in diameter, that inches across the back of the stage, higher than the dancers. When it reaches the center, the stage is suddenly bathed in strong white light that visually obliterates the scrim until there is an equally sudden return to the initial murkiness. One quality that separates *Inlets* from other recent work and yet connects it to my earlier favorites is a fuller exploitation of theatrical resources.

Whenever Cunningham appears on stage nowadays, he gets an extra round of applause (as did Gordie Howe in his reborn years), but (as with Howe) one wonders whether these fans are honoring him in the present or appreciating his career which, as everyone knows by now, has had the classic avant-garde shape of early innovation that his elders dismissed, professional exclusion, sustained productivity in spite of public incomprehension and financial hardships, the development of a loyal nucleus of colleagues and then an expanding, loyal, proselytizing audience, and finally a breakthrough into popular acclaim.

The difference is that Cunningham two decades ago made us think about the possibilities of dance and of the theater. There was a spikey edge to his work and to its relationship to the audience. I find that challenging quality—that risk of unacceptability—still in much of John Cage's recent work, which is at times outrageous and can drive out audiences; I find a bit of that sort of edge in Cunningham's work with film and video. (There might be even more of such an edge in choreography for *objects*, the dance equivalent of electronic music, were he to think about doing it.)

At the root of his creative predicament is, paradoxically, his company—or, rather, the pragmatic and ultimately esthetic burdens of supporting his talented entourage, which is the professional convention that Cunningham shares with his more conservative colleagues; and now that the company is so strong, and so much larger than before, while invitations remain plentiful, he is even more beholden to it. Nonetheless, isn't it reasonable to speculate about what would happen to his art if he freed himself of that baggage?

John Cage

GRACE AND CLARITY (1944)

The strength that comes from firmly established art practices is not present in the modern dance today. Insecure, not having any clear direction, the modern dancer is willing to compromise and to accept influences from other more rooted art manners, enabling one to remark that certain dancers are either borrowing from or selling themselves to Broadway, others are learning from folk and Oriental arts, and many are either introducing into their work elements of the ballet, or, in an all-out effort, devoting themselves to it. Confronted with its history, its former power, its present insecurity, the realization is unavoidable that the strength the modern dance once had was not impersonal but was intimately connected with and ultimately dependent on the personalities and even the actual physical bodies of the individuals who imparted it.

The techniques of the modern dance were once orthodox. It did not enter a dancer's mind that they might be altered. To add to them was the sole privilege of the originators.

Intensive summer courses were the scenes of the new dispensations, reverently transmitted by the master-students. When the fanatically followed leaders began, and when they continued, to desert their own teachings (adapting chiefly balletish movements to their own rapidly-growing-less-rigorous techniques), a general and profound insecurity fell over the modern dance.

Where any strength now exists in the modern dance, it is, as before, in isolated personalities and physiques. In the case of the young, this is unfortunate; for, no matter how impressive and revelatory their expressed outlooks on life are, they are overshadowed, in the minds of audiences, and often, grown in stature; in *Nocturnes* Viola Farber and Mr. Charlip also move to the fore, and I must also mention John Cage's performance of the Satie, which can only be indicated as "ideal" or "inevitable."

Sets and costumes by Bob Rauschenberg displayed a verve and unerring taste which one could only expect from him. The lighting for the Cunningham recital was by Nicola Cernovich, who has no small part in the general success.

Two Reviews (1960–63) by Jill Johnston

1960

With three works new to New York, Merce Cunningham appeared at the Phoenix Theatre the evening of February 16. The only dance "old" to New York was *Changeling*, performed November 1957, his solo in bright red. But one performance two years and four months ago does not make it so old; it would in fact take a number of performances to make a Cunningham dance seem very old, and even then it would probably seem old only because of the number of times it had been performed, not because it had grown tiresome through familiarity.

There is much to see in a dance by Cunningham. *Summerspace* (1958) and *Rune* (1959) are teeming with the ever-shifting patterns and designs that he creates in his dances for group. Imagine sitting in a room where two large and complicated paintings are on exhibition; but instead of reposing in their conventional stationary positions, they are passed slowly through the room, in one door and out the other, and that is all you see of them. You would probably retain the impression of the dominant color tones, the general shape and texture, and the pervasive "mood." But you would feel like returning to the room to examine all the details and the way everything fits together.

Well, *Rune* is a very large and complicated dance. It would be good to see it again soon. It is a Grand dance, statuesque, and almost heroic. It contains some typically swift and dazzling passages, but the dominant tone is a rich, slow brown. By contrast, *Summerspace* is light and resilient, a "lyric dance," the program says. It is bounding and spacious with air. And it has the quality of the speckled backdrop and costumes—something like the dappled play of light and shadow caused by the sun when it glints through leaves.

Antic Meet (1958) is not so difficult to see at one sitting, perhaps because each incident has a special character and makes an indelible impression— indelibly funny. What a superb joke, these episodic "take-offs" on the dance, with inserted nonsense! It is not really so important that the dance is mostly a spoof of various kinds of dancing; the idea provides a good excuse for a wonderful collection of absurdities. And except for two or three numbers, you can't be too certain what is a take-off on what. Anyway, it does include: a delicate ballet farce between two girls called "Sports and Diversions #1"; another "Sports and Diversions #2" in which the two men romp around in a kind of athletic competition, ending with Mr. Cunningham in a raccoon coat, dragging off a defeated Mr. Charlip; a mechanically efficient solo by Viola Farber carrying an umbrella with a spray of lights under it, which could be a nightclub act; a wonderful "Social" for everybody in dark eyeglasses with a femme-fatale ending (you might miss it, but Marilyn Wood puts a death grip on Mr. Charlip as they exit); "Room for Two," a bedroom farce, I believe, which includes a door, a nightgown (on Carolyn Brown), and a chair strapped on a back; Mr. Cunningham as Bacchus in a big sweater with several arms, dancing with several cohorts (including Judith Dunn)—a number which someone tells me is a take-off on Martha Graham; a charming soft-shoe dance by Mr. Cunningham, whimsically understated; and an "Opener" and "Exodus" which *could* be a spoof by Mr. Cunningham on himself . . . ?

1963

During the intermission at José Limón's recent concert in [New York's] Philharmonic Hall someone observed that Limón's art is for middlebrows. The observer meant that his dances are easy to grasp. In "The Traitor" there is a bad man and a kind of saint, and nobody could doubt the issue. Moreover, the embodiment of good and evil in the figures of Christ and Judas could hardly escape any Western spectator, since the symbolism is explicit and complete. Limón has never been a subtle artist. If you don't get it the first time he'll hammer it out a few more times. The dance distortions never veer far from the broad representational gesture. The choral movements emphasize the solo drama. The narrative proceeds in logical sequence. So altogether the audience is permitted to feel quite comfortable. That must account for the packed house at Philharmonic Hall.

By contrast, the audience the previous week for Merce Cunningham, although substantial enough, was far from packed. I learned from *The New York Times* that more people would turn up if they didn't have to hear John Cage's music. The implication in the *Times* was that Cunningham himself is okay but that he ought to get rid of Cage if he wants to appeal to the outlying districts. That's like asking Limón to throw down the Bible, although nobody would suggest it, because the Bible is a big drawing card in the outlying districts. I don't mean to equate Cage with the Bible. What I'm saying is that the collaboration of Cage and Cunningham makes perfect sense and that it is as difficult to conceive of Cunningham without Cage's music (and direction) as it is to imagine Limón without his literature.

In any event, Cage is not the only deterrent in this matter of popularity. Cunningham's dances are still beyond the general public because he doesn't give the public anything literal to hold on to. His dances are all about movement, and what you see in them that relates to your common experience is your own business and not his.

The dance world is embarrassingly backward. Cunningham should pack

Five (1956) the actions—now gay, now anguished, now grotesque—are as diverse as nature herself; yet in being purged of causation they are purged too of the nag of memory and the tug of desire. This they achieve *through* their lack of relationship to Cage's music, which is even more devoid of progression or motor-rhythm than is Japanese temple music. The softly reverberative sounds of the prepared piano—occurring at chronometric points dictated by chance operations, and separated by immense silences—really do cause one to listen anew: while Rauschenberg's almost-blank costumes and decor help one to see the actions with unblinkered eyes.

Crises (1960), as the title suggests, is less abstract, more dramatic, though the erotic implications of these actions between a man and four women evade climax. The music is Conlon Nancarrow's celebrated studies for three player-pianos. The fantastic complexity of the polyrhythms, which machines can negotiate when human beings couldn't, transmutes the sexy and nostalgic flavour of jazz and pop into loony hysteria. Yet the sounds preserve, in their mechanisation, a disembodied detachment, and this communicates itself to the actions. For all the sleaziness of the atmosphere and the violence of the gestures, we are released from our more inchoate appetites in simply accepting them. Even they can take their place with "the permanent emotions of Indian tradition"; and Merce Cunningham's [untitled] *Solo* (1953) to Christian Wolff's pianistic explosions goes still further, for it induces a therapeutic calm from the neurotic twitch and spastic shiver that (at least since *West Side Story*) we've come to recognise as gestures typical of our world and time.

Story (1963), with background noises derived from the audible universe by Toshi Ichiyanagi, is the least abstract of these ballets. Here Rauschenberg comes into his own, for there is a setting (a television studio), and the dancers, inspiring one another to variously indeterminate activities, bring in an assortment of Rauschenbergian "objects." The ballet consists of "happenings," executed, however, by dancers of great technical skills. While the result is dadaistically hilarious, it's by no means only that. The pathos of the clown figures reminded me of Satie's *Parade*, for which Cunningham could and should do a superb new choreography. It's a pity that the large and on the whole enthusiastic audience decided in advance that this piece was to be an unmitigated hoot; though it's only fair to add that they remained rapt during the longest and stillest silences of *Suite for Five*.

Merce Cunningham

SPACE, TIME AND DANCE
(1952)

The dance is an art in space and time.
The object of the dancer is to obliterate that.

The classical ballet, by maintaining the image of the Renaissance perspective in stage thought, kept a linear form of space. The modern American dance, stemming from German expressionism and the personal feelings of the various American pioneers, made space into a series of lumps, or often just static hills on the stage with actually no relation to the larger space of the stage area, but simply forms that by their connection in time made a shape. Some of the space-thought coming from a German dance opened the space out, and left a momentary feeling of connection with it, but too often the space was not visible enough because the physical action was all of a lightness, like sky without earth, or heaven without hell.

The fortunate thing in dancing is that space and time cannot be disconnected, and everyone can see and understand that. A body still is taking up just as much space and time as a body moving. The result is that neither the one nor the other—moving or being still—is more or less important, except it's nice to see a dancer moving. But the moving becomes more clear if the space and time around the moving are one of its opposites—stillness. Aside from the personal skill and clarity of the individual dancer, there are certain things that make clear to a spectator what the dancer is doing. In the ballet, the various steps that lead to the larger movements or poses have, by usage and by their momentum, become common ground upon which the spectator can lead his

37

eyes and his feelings into the resulting action. This also helps define the rhythm, in fact more often than not does define it. In the modern dance, the tendency or the wish has been to get rid of these "unnecessary and balletic" movements, at the same time wanting the same result in the size and vigor of the movement as the balletic action, and this has often left the dancer and the spectator slightly short.

To quibble with that on the other side: one of the best discoveries the modern dance has made use of is the gravity of the body in weight, that is, as opposite from denying (and thus affirming) gravity by ascent into the air, the weight of the body in going with gravity, down. The word "heavy" connotes something incorrect, since what is meant is not the heaviness of a bag of cement falling, although we've all been spectators of that too, but the heaviness of a living body falling with full intent of eventual rise. This is not a fetish or a use of heaviness as an accent against a predominantly light quality, but a thing in itself. By its nature this kind of moving would make the space seem a series of unconnected spots, along with the lack of clear-connecting movements in the modern dance.

A prevalent feeling among many painters that lets them make a space in which anything can happen is a feeling dancers may have too. Imitating the way nature makes a space and puts lots of things in it, heavy and light, little and big, all unrelated, yet each affecting all the others.

About the formal methods of choreography—some due to the conviction that a communication of one order or another is necessary; others to the feeling that mind follows heart, that is, form follows content; some due to the feeling that the musical form is the most logical to follow—the most curious to me is the general feeling in the modern dance that nineteenth-century forms stemming from earlier pre-classical forms are the only formal actions advisable, or even possible to take. This seems a flat contradiction of the modern dance—agreeing with the thought of discovering new or allegedly new movement for contemporary reasons, the using of psychology as a tremendous elastic basis for content, and wishing to be expressive of the "times" (although how can one be expressive of anything else)—but not feeling the need for a different basis upon which to put this expression, in fact being mainly content to indicate that either the old forms are good enough, or further that the old forms are the only possible forms. These consist mainly of theme and variation, and associated devices—repetition, inversion, development, and manipulation. There is also a tendency to imply a crisis to which one goes and then in some way retreats from. Now I can't see that crisis any longer means a climax, unless we are willing to grant that every breath of wind has a climax (which I am), but then that obliterates climax, being a surfeit of such. And since our lives, both by nature by the newspapers are so full of crisis that one is no longer aware of it, then it is clear that life goes on regardless, and further that each thing can be and is separate from each and every other, viz: the continuity of the newspaper headlines. Climax is for those who are swept by New Year's Eve.

More freeing into *space* than the theme and manipulation "holdup" would be a formal structure based on *time*. Now time can be an awful lot of bother with the ordinary pinch-penny counting that has to go on with it, but if one can think of the structure as a space of time in which anything can happen in any sequence of movement event, and any length of stillness can take place, then the counting is an aid towards freedom, rather than a discipline towards mechanization. A use of time-structure also frees the music into space, making the connection between the dance and the music one of individual autonomy connected at structural points. The result is the dance is free to act as it chooses, as is the music. The music doesn't have to work itself to death to underline the dance, or the dance create havoc in trying to be as flashy as the music.

For me, it seems enough that dancing is a spiritual exercise in physical form, and that what is seen, is what it is. And I do not believe it is possible to be "too simple." What the dancer does is the most realistic of all possible things, and to pretend that a man standing on a hill could be doing everything except just standing is simply divorce—divorce from life, from the sun coming up and going down, from clouds in front of the sun, from the rain that comes from the clouds and sends you into the drugstore for a cup of coffee, from each thing that succeeds each thing. Dancing is a visible action of life.

Remy Charlip

COMPOSING BY CHANCE (1954)

Merce Cunningham's suite, *Sixteen Dances for Soloist and Company of Three* (1951) when last performed at the Alvin Theatre, produced a lively, controversial reaction. Programmed between the familiar *Appalachian Spring* of Martha Graham and *The Moor's Pavane* of José Limón, the response was immediate. After each of the sixteen dances there were boos and applause, cheers and hisses. The dances were simply titled, "Solo," "Duet," "Trio," or "Quartet," and followed one another without any apparent story or thematic coherence. The music, movement, and costumes, as well as the continuity, were unfamiliar.

One of the ideas that prompted these dances is to be found in the traditional Hindu theory of the *rasas* or permanent emotions. The *rasas* number nine. Four are white: the Erotic, the Heroic, the Mirthful, and the Wondrous. Four are black: Fear, the Odious, Anger, and Sorrow. The ninth, neither white nor black, but essential to both, and often described as special to the performer's art, is Tranquillity. The aspect of impermanence or sentimentality has been attributed to other emotional qualities than those given above.

Using this as a starting point, Mr. Cunningham choreographed a continuity of individual dances, a dance using a permanent emotion to be followed by one using an impermanent emotion. This, of course, was a structural idea, and need not interfere with anyone's own direct emotional response to each dance. For example, dance number 9, a solo, in which Mr. Cunningham wears a huge colorful coat, and makes use of vocal sounds, shouts, groans, and grunts, there seems, to this writer, to be an emphasis on the Heroic, with the Mirthful and the Odious also present; whereas, Mr. Cunningham used as a starting point only the Odious. Reactions are naturally various. Some see this dance as a hunter frightened by his hunt, others as an exuberant drunk on a binge.

The music and the costumes have a formal arrangement, which allows for a single change for each dance. In the music, John Cage started with a specific set of sixty-four sounds for the first dance, and for each pair of dances replaced eight sounds with eight others, until at the end there was a completely new set of sounds. The first piece started with harsh and sharp sounds, and in the last piece there were long and resounding sounds. The costumes were treated in a similar manner, with dark and warm colors in the beginning, and with one costume change for each dance, ending in cool, light colors in order to contribute to the final, serene effect.

Mr. Cunningham's arrangement of the sequence of dances was based on the conviction that it is possible for anything to follow anything else, and that the actual order of events can be chanced rather than chosen, the resultant experience being free and discovered, rather than bound and remembered.

The chance method of choreography can clearly be seen in a later work which will have its New York premiere on December 29th called *Suite by Chance*. It is a long dance in four movements to music for magnetic tape by Christian Wolff. For this dance, a large series of charts was made: a chart numbering body movements of various kinds (phrases and positions, in movement and in stillness); a chart numbering lengths of time (so that a phrase or position could be done in a long or short duration, or, in the case of the impossibility of lengthening the time of a movement, as, for instance, a single step, it could be repeated for the length of time given); a chart numbering directions in space (floor plans).

These charts, which defined the physical limits within which the continuity would take place, were not made by chance. But from them, with a method similar to one used in a lottery, the actual continuity was found. That is, a sequence of movements for a single dancer was determined by means of chance from the numbered movements in the chart; space, direction, and lengths of time were found in the other charts. At important structural points in the music, the number of dancers on stage, exits and entrances, unison or individual movements of dancers were all decided by tossing coins. In this way, a dancer may be standing still one moment, leaping or spinning the next. There are familiar and unfamiliar movements, but what is continuously unfamiliar is the continuity, freed as it is from usual cause and effect relations. Due to the chance method, some of the movements listed in the charts were used more than once in different space and directions and for different lengths of time, and, on the other hand, many movements, to be found in the charts, do not appear at all in the final choreography.

For each new dance a new set of charts is made listing movements that Mr. Cunningham is interested in using at the time of composing.

Calvin Tomkins

ON COLLABORATION (1974)

> *You have to love dancing to stick to it. It gives nothing back, no*
> *manuscripts to store away, no paintings to show on the walls and maybe*
> *hang in museums, no poems to be printed and sold, nothing but that*
> *single fleeting moment when you feel alive.*
>
> Merce Cunningham

Twenty years ago, when Merce Cunningham's first company was still evolving from an occasional association into a seasoned performing unit, Cunningham asked Robert Rauschenberg to design a set for a new dance called *Minutiae* (1954). It was not the first time Cunningham had collaborated with a visual artist—Isamu Noguchi had done the set for *The Seasons*, a Cunningham ballet commissioned in 1947 by Lincoln Kirstein's newly-formed Ballet Society; David Hare had designed a costume for a Cunningham solo dance in 1945 (it proved too heavy to wear); and Remy Charlip had done the costumes for a number of Cunningham's early dances. But in commissioning Rauschenberg, Cunningham had in mind a different sort of working arrangement.

"The dance was not finished," Cunningham recalls. "I said to Bob, 'I don't want you to decorate a dance, but to make something that we could use *in* a dance.' He made an object, and beautiful as it was it wouldn't work, because it needed a pipe to hang on. So he made a second one through which we walked, huddled, and climbed. It was very fragile, with lots of lace, and comic strips, and a little hanging mirror. It was like an object in nature which hadn't been named." This was the beginning of an association that lasted for eleven years, during which Rauschenberg made the sets or costumes (or both) for twenty-four Cunningham dances, and also toured with the company as its lighting designer. It now appears inevitable that Cunningham, who over the years has commissioned scores for his dances by most of the leading avant-garde composers, should also have wanted to work with artists such as Rauschenberg, Jasper Johns, Frank Stella, Andy Warhol, Robert Morris, and Bruce Nauman. Far more than any other choreographer in our time, Cunningham has pursued the difficult goal of a true synthesis of the arts, and the manner of his doing so, I believe, has a bearing not only on his own remarkable career but on the development of twentieth-century art.

It is necessary to remember that for Cunningham, collaboration never implies the subordination of one art to another. It was Cunningham and John Cage, since 1953 the musical director of the Cunningham company, who first broke with the tradition that the music in a dance performance had to support the dance (or, conversely, that the dance should "interpret" the music). Cunningham and Cage have always proceeded on the basis that music and dance are two separate activities taking place within the same time sequence, and, in a Cunningham dance, neither depends upon the other. The same process applies to the artists who design sets for Cunningham. Consultations between artist and choreographer determine a few general guidelines, such as the dimensions of the stage, and sometimes the kinds of movement to be expected, but after that the artist goes off to his studio and makes the set while Cunningham makes the dance, and usually the two come together only during the final rehearsals.

Curiously enough, this seemingly "blind" form of collaboration does not engender catastrophes. The Cunningham dancers move with their customary precision through the brilliant maze of Stella's stretched canvas strips (in *Scramble* [1967]), or among Warhol's floating silver pillows (in *RainForest* [1968]); they are no more put off by Morris's moving column of light (*Canfield* [1969]) or by Nauman's phalanx of electric fans (*Tread* [1970]) than they are by the electronic and "found" sounds of Cage, Morton Feldman, Christian Wolff, Toshi Ichiyanagi, or La Monte Young. Movement, music, and decor coexist in the same stage space and the same performance time, and the result—what is the result? Not a melding of these elements into a unified spectacle, not that at all. It is closer in feeling to collage, in which disparate elements are brought together without becoming fused. We, the spectators, are invited to pay attention on three levels simultaneously, to hold in mind three separate forms and all the subtle reverberations among them. The result is as complex, as demanding, and as full of surprises as anything in our experience. If we are sufficiently alert, it can also be indistinguishable from "that single fleeting moment when you feel alive."

In its early years, the Cunningham company's New York performances attracted more painters and sculptors than musicians or dancers. A benefit sale of paintings by New York artists helped to make possible the company's first world tour in 1964; two years later, when the company was invited to take part in the Paris International Dance Festival and the State Department refused to pay a nickel toward its travel expenses (Cunningham was still too "controversial"), the trip was financed through the sale of a painting donated for that purpose by Joan Miró. The fact that so many contemporary artists have admired Cunningham's work to the point of supporting it financially may suggest that they also sensed in it a certain affinity to their own. Certainly Cunningham's feeling that dance movement could be presented for its own sake—not to express ideas or emotions or to tell stories—has its clear parallel in Rauschenberg's wish to work as a sort of "collaborator" with his materials, as well as with the efforts of Morris Louis, Ellsworth Kelly, and others to liberate color from any nonchromatic reference. The "all-over" paintings of Jackson Pollock and others of his generation had helped Cunningham to arrive at his own method of making dances in which there is no single center of interest ("Any part of the stage is interesting, can be used," as Cunningham says). And in their use of chance methods to go beyond self-expression, Cunningham and Cage went much further along the road travelled earlier by the surrealists and to a certain extent by the abstract expressionists. The surrealists saw chance as a means of allowing the subconscious mind to assert itself directly in art. For Cage and Cunningham, on the other hand, chance offered a possible means to outdistance the self entirely—subconscious and all—and to get into a new field of human awareness in which every part of the terrain was unfamiliar.

The new set of demands that work of this kind made and makes upon the spectator was prefigured, of course, in the life and work of Marcel Duchamp, who still enrages traditionalist critics by emerging, ever more clearly since his death, as the most influential artist of the century. It was Duchamp, speaking as a "mere artist" in 1957, who proposed that the artist should be seen as a "mediumistic being" who performed only one part of the creative process, and that it was up to the spectator to decipher and interpret the work's inner qualifications, relate them to his own experience, and thus complete the creative cycle. Every dance by Cunningham invites this sort of participation, and in recent years his audiences have proved more and more willing to accept the compliment thus paid them. Each person is free to interpret each dance as he sees fit, or not to interpret it at all. A work such as *Winterbranch* (1964), for example, with its random patterns of light and darkness on stage and its falling movements, has impressed various people as being "about" nuclear war, concentration camps, or Vietnam—it once struck the wife of a sea captain as being about shipwreck. *Walkaround Time* (1968), the hour-long piece that Cunningham made in homage to Duchamp, and for which Jasper Johns designed a set derived from Duchamp's *Large Glass* in Philadelphia, has seemed to this observer a strikingly different dance each time he has seen it. Cunningham himself does not think that his dances are "about" anything, but he is willing to accept the fact that others may find specific ways to interpret them. As he wrote some years ago, "If the dancer dances—which is not the same as having theories about dancing or wishing to dance or trying to dance or remembering in his body someone else's dance—but if the dancer *dances,* everything is there. The meaning is there if that's what you want."

Cage once expressed the idea that at certain periods, one of the arts does the talking while the others listen. During the fifties and the early sixties in New York, he said, painting clearly was doing the talking. Is it possible now that dance has become the main speaker? The proliferation of modern dance and ballet companies not only in New York but throughout the country, the rapid growth in the audience—according to a recent Ford Foundation report, dance now outdraws rock music on college campuses—and the overflowing classes at schools such as Cunningham's all point to some such conclusion. One might also note the number of contemporary artists and composers who seem drawn today in the direction of "performance" or "process" pieces that depend to a large extent on movement and gesture of one kind or another, and the recent developments in theater—Peter Brook's international experiments, for example, or Robert Wilson's spectacles in extended time—whose real roots are in the dance and the body's natural expressiveness. How much these developments owe to Cunningham is anyone's guess (Brook and Wilson have both acknowledged their enthusiasm for his work). What is certain in any case is that for more than twenty years, the immense creative energy generated first by Cunningham, Cage, and Rauschenberg working together, and after 1966 by Cunningham, Cage, and Jasper Johns (who became the company's artistic advisor in that year) has been among the strongest forces at work in the arts, here and abroad, and that it shows no sign of losing momentum.

Cunningham's influence is all indirect, like that of Zen master who goes on doing what he does. "I don't think I've ever demanded particular things," he said the other day, referring to his work with visual artists. "My ideas about dancing are all so flexible, and working with artists has made them more so. I could just as well tell people to go and dance in a field, with or without a tree—it would be nice if there were a tree, but not essential. So many people think that decor should emphasize something, or define it, or frame it some-how, but life doesn't work that way, and I don't either. I grew up with this business of dance movements meaning something specific, but it always seemed to me that a movement could mean a lot of different things, and that it didn't make much sense to act like a dictator."

Not one center but a multiplicity of centers, connected and equal in value. Cunningham and Cage are there in that expanding field of awareness (with or without a tree) and we are there with them, if we are lucky. This is the new situation. And as Cage would say, it is simply delightful.

nothing else)—had a long conversation. In fact, Carolyn, John, and I had such a vibrant meeting and conversation that we sort of dominated the evening, which made everybody else at the party rather angry.

Then there was a master class at Jane McLean's, and I remember seeing Merce's eyes watching Carolyn do diagonals from one corner of the studio to another. I don't think he expected to meet a dancer like Carolyn in Denver, but to this day I can see Merce looking up as if he were saying, "Where did *that* come from?"

So it was a good meeting, for Merce and Carolyn as dancers and for John and me as composers. And we had marvelous conversations at two or three parties on different nights.

Then John saw my music. I sent some early work, *Three Pieces for Piano*, which I wrote in 1951, to John in New York, and he gave them to David Tudor, and that led to the first performance of any music of mine in New York. That was at the Cherry Lane Theater, under the auspices of the Living Theater, later in 1951.

After the Brandeis festival and the Black Mountain summer of '52, Carolyn and I moved to New York. John had invited me to work with him and David Tudor on what John called *Project for Music for Magnetic Tape*. I believe he was inspired to start that kind of project after hearing the Schaeffer-Henry *Symphonie* at Brandeis. Anyway, John invited me, and Merce was quite obviously pleased to have Carolyn arrive too. This must have been about September 1952. And there began an extraordinary kind of friendship and collaboration: learning, arguing—John and myself especially arguing. Carolyn began taking classes with Merce, and also at Juilliard, and soon after joined the Cunningham company.

MARIANNE SIMON: The company coalesced at Black Mountain the following summer.

BROWN: The first piece of mine that Merce used, I wrote for him. He used two other of my pieces, but the work I wrote for him was *Indices* for chamber orchestra, seventeen or eighteen instruments, and *Springweather and People* (1955) was danced to it. Didn't it have costumes and scenery by Remy?

REMY CHARLIP: No scenery, just costumes. I conceived it, and it was a collaboration of several people.

BROWN: I remember there were big parachutes. Looped.

CHARLIP: It was fan-pleated silk.

BROWN: The music and the dance were twenty-nine minutes long. That's a lot of music. *Why* I did it is important. I was writing a piece for Merce in order to pay for Carolyn's dance classes, because we had no money. John and David and I were getting forty dollars a week each, working on the tape music project, so we didn't have much extra money. I knew way in front that I would have only one hour of rehearsal for a piece twenty-nine minutes long. That means twice through, if you're lucky.

The other two works of mine that Merce used, but which I didn't write for him, were from a collection called *Folio*, composed between 1952 and 1954. He set *Galaxy* (1956) on *Four Systems*. I believe that was the first time Merce had done an open-form dance, in the sense of spontaneous performance.

I was not at all interested in composing by chance. I was far more interested in spontaneity and immediacy and directness. I usually wrote all of my material subjectively (and that's a long story), making what I called mobile scores, mobile musical pieces, which Europeans later called "open-form." That means the music can begin anywhere and go from that point to any other point within my composed materials. *Four Systems* was a graphic piece which, as a matter of fact, I wrote backstage at the Brooklyn Academy of Music, where Merce's company was performing. Merce, I guess, said, "We're having a party for David Tudor's birthday tonight at the studio," which was then on Sheridan Square in the Village. John and I glanced at each other. Neither of us had remembered that it was David's birthday; we didn't have any presents for him. So John and I looked around backstage. I found a scrap of cardboard big enough to sketch a little music on. John found some cardboard, too, or some kind of paper, and he punched holes in it, by chance, I suppose. Under any conditions he always had three pennies to flip, except in Chinese restaurants, when he usually *chose* his menu.

Anyway, John punched out a piece which was his first music for carillon, I believe. I called my piece *Four Systems*. And those were the birthday presents we gave David Tudor at the studio party that night. David performed my piece long before Merce choreographed to it.

That is how the music for *Galaxy* came to be. I'd like to know if it was the first—and only—time Merce choreographed an open-form work. Four people were in it: Carolyn, Viola Farber, Marianne, and Remy. Their material was choreographed but, as in my music, they could enter at any time they wanted. I believe it was the first spontaneous—

CHARLIP: I don't remember doing anything spontaneous in Merce's dances. Maybe the entrances were. The piece itself was set.

BROWN: In form?

CHARLIP: Yes. I mean, there was always that big argument about spontaneity.

BROWN: But if the entrances are not fixed, how can the form be fixed?

CHARLIP: Well, I remember going through my whole solo, the length of time that it was. I don't remember changing the order of what I did.

BROWN: But they could overlap in different ways?

CHARLIP: I guess so.

VAUGHAN: Each person had a solo. Didn't Merce, essentially, make four solos that were performed at the same time?

CHARLIP: We were the four elements. I was Fire. Marianne was Earth. Carolyn was Air. I made the costumes for it, and Carolyn had mesh hose on him to get brake drums. It was a sight, Lou going around this junkyard and hitting brake drums to try to find the right note for his piece.

John invented the "prepared piano" by putting things into an ordinary piano to make the sounds come from other than what we think of as musical sources. Or using the sources differently, as Henry Cowell did, by strumming the wires inside of the piano or banging one's whole arm down on the keys. Later, John would slam down the lid to gain that sound.

Bonnie Bird once asked John, "What can I do to make music for children?" John said, "Why don't you have them play the room?"

SIMON: I met Merce in Paris when I was nineteen, in the early summer of 1949. I saw him perform a piece in a studio so small that it only had about four feet of space, and there were maybe thirty people sitting around the four feet. He was dancing with Tanaquil LeClercq and Betty Nichols. I was very excited, especially when I heard that Merce was staying in the same hotel as a friend of mine and was looking for a studio (the studio where he performed was not one he taught in). So I sat outside the hotel about four hours waiting for Merce to appear, and when he did I said breathlessly, "I hear you need a studio." That was the extent of my eloquence, unlike Earle's and Carolyn's when they met John. But Merce took the studio I told him about, and that's how I got to know him.

He returned to the States about the same time I did, and he started a class because he wanted to train people to dance the way he danced. I was the first student—in fact, the *only* student in the class for a couple of weeks, until Remy joined. After the first class Merce said, "OK, get into position." I did. And he said, "Now jump." I couldn't get off the floor. That was my beginning, quite different from Carolyn's.

In this first group that he was training himself, to Merce it was of the utmost importance that he use dancers who didn't have preconceived ideas about how movement was supposed to look. Why that was important became evident as we went on. Merce was developing movement that other choreographers were not, and he found it confining to use dancers who'd been trained by others and who had mannerisms and certain ways of going about dance.

About four months after the class began we gave a program at Cooper Union. Six of us did *Rag-Time Parade* (1950), which he'd originally made for untrained dancers. He called us his junior company, and we were not at all skillful. *Rag-Time* was outfitted from Second Avenue thrift shops, and it was quite wild and wonderful and funny. The other dancers in the class, whom we called the senior company, did *A Diversion* (1948). We got an encore and they didn't. So that was a wonderful introduction.

After the Brandeis festival, he stopped using dancers whom other people had trained, but by then we were good enough to become the senior company. He was beginning to make unique dances, although *Rag-Time* was quite unusual.

We underwent many shocks in the process of learning his choreography. *Springweather* was the most unusual score we had yet danced to. Merce was convinced that there was no way we could ever figure out from the score where we were to be or how to get together at different moments. After a while he asked, "How is it that you keep being together at these different times?" We said, "Well, we have musical cues." Except that we didn't, in the accepted sense. In our naîveté, we listened to whatever sound was presented and heard it as music and used it the way we would have traditionally. Hearing a squeak or a beep, we'd know that we were supposed to be in a certain part of the stage. Merce was quite surprised at our ingenuity.

Even then his way of dancing was very different from traditional modern dance, which was mostly Limón and Graham. Whether he was influenced by Zen then, I don't know. But what we learned was that we were doing just what we were doing and never anything else. It had nothing to do with drama or mental images or emotional responses. It had to do with our learning to be exactly where we were when we were there, doing what we were supposed to be doing. Merce insisted that we be very precise, that our movement be exactly the way it was supposed to look, that we fit into the frame of time the way we were supposed to; and to ensure that we always danced up to tempo, he made us move quickly and very lightly.

In secret, of course, we'd make up elaborate stories about what was actually going on. He'd laugh when we told him these scenarios, but they didn't bother him so long as they didn't intrude on his dynamics and timing.

CHARLIP: Once Merce was rehearsing a solo which absolutely freaked me out. I thought he was having a fit and said to John, "He's not going to do that in public, is he?" It was so amazing that it made possible my realization that I could do something as personal and intense, too. Particularly in his solos, what he danced was directly in touch with his feelings and had immediate emotional content. The group dances were quite different. He wouldn't tell us what they were about.

SIMON: He would deny that they were about anything, but we knew better.

A difference I've noticed between the early dances, particularly *Springweather and People*, and the dances now, is that when he was beginning to make chance dances there was an enormous amount of stillness. In *Springweather* we must have stood for fifteen minutes in one corner of the stage, four of us, doing nothing—actually, we were doing something: we were being still. But that seems to have vanished from Merce's dances today.

VAUGHAN: A little of the stillness is coming back, actually. It's one of those ingredients that goes away but returns.

The period when you were rehearsing both *Les Noces* and the *Symphonie pour un homme seul* (both 1952), utterly different pieces—was there a clear difference in the way Merce was making them?

Sometimes David Tudor would be there to play, and sometimes not. But we didn't really learn a piece to the music at all.

VAUGHAN: Of course you know the wonderful story about *Banjo*, that you rehearsed it sometimes with a pianist at Black Mountain who wasn't David Tudor. And everybody was wondering why they were dancing to this rather ordinary piece of jangly Gottschalk music, until Merce asked David Tudor if he would mind playing it once for the dancers, since he was going to play for the performance. David, in an extraordinary exhibition of virtuosity, really made the music sound like a dozen banjos, and the dancers understood why Merce wanted to use that music.

CHARLIP: What we were doing began to influence others. Up at Columbia, John did a piece of music for twelve radios, and I was one of the dial twisters. Then Jimmy Waring did *Dances Before the Wall* (1957). The wall was a gorgeous set by Julian Beck. Jimmy took his favorite pieces of music, cut them up to different lengths, and matched them with the different lengths of his dances. A dance got going, and right in the middle of it a new piece of music might start and go through to the middle of the next dance, when the music would switch to another piece, which could be everything from classical to popular music to sounds of dishes breaking. The dance, one of Jimmy's most beautiful, was the first by anyone but Merce to use the concept that you have the dancers follow your choreography but continually and arbitrarily change their music in the middle of the dancing. Of course Paul Taylor and others have choreographed a dance to one piece of music but performed it to another. Toby Armour made a dance she showed twice, once in silence and once with music. Some choreographers make different dances to the same music. So the concept of music and dance becomes wide open.

SIMON: From the dancer's point of view, the work we did on being extremely precise, doing the movements exactly the way we were taught, within the time frame imposed, at the speed that Merce insisted upon—perfecting all of this made it immaterial whether music or sound accompanied us. If we continually did Cunningham movement exactly the way we were supposed to, our bodies learned how much time a movement needed and automatically took up the right amount of time.

BROWN: That's why I called my notation "time notation." I believed a musician could have a kinesthetic memory as keen as a dancer's, which I'd seen confirmed by Cunningham's people working in that way.

VAUGHAN: The surrealists, whose work Merce would have seen in Paris and even earlier in New York, used chance. Did this influence him at all?

BROWN: One of the definitions of surrealism is that it's the simultaneous occurrence of mutually disparate objects, which is to say that anything can follow anything. That aspect of the surrealists' revolution influenced me—not to the extent of using chance, as Merce did, but the way it opened my whole world to events relating to each other just by being there.

CHARLIP: Surrealism to me is simply landscapes as portraiture, portraiture as still life, still life as landscape. It frees your seeing. The dadaists widened that freedom. Jean Arp dropped pieces of paper from above and glued them where they landed. Artists later covered the body with paint and pressed against canvas. In Japan, the Gutai Group, who predated the Black Mountain Happening, combined simultaneous events and juxtaposed space and activities. I was fascinated by a mud dance they did. We were aware of and influenced by all of these things.

BROWN: The Gutai were highly spontaneous; it was like action painting. People tearing through a series of brown paper frames. And that was a work of art. It was performed in front of you, and then it stood as a result.

VAUGHAN: Merce and John were also aware of what was occurring in American painting at this period; for instance, the way Jackson Pollock used space.

CHARLIP: Yes, just dripping something on the floor and that's what it is. Not conceiving anything beforehand. In one of my first conversations with John—I had just come out of Cooper Union—we talked about a concept new to me that I had learned: of how thrilling the surface of canvas and the matter of paint is, that it is the material one is working with that's of the utmost interest rather than what you're trying to say with it. For the first time I had realized that a canvas might be interesting whether it was covered with white paint or was left free, raw. And what is the surface? What does the surface mean in relation to when you put paint on it? These concepts were reflected in John's punching holes in a piece of paper to indicate notes for his music, or drawing a graph on ordinary blank paper and holding it up to the light, which would reveal imperfections in the paper. And those places were where John put his notes on the graph.

VAUGHAN: *Suite for Five in Space and Time* (1956) was done to music written that way; and Merce used the same process in making the choreography, to determine where in the stage space the dancers would be positioned. I believe there was a page for each of the dances.

CHARLIP: Yes. Take a page keyed to areas of the stage, hold it up to the light, and the imperfection you see within the sheet of paper places the dancers on the stage.

I was so excited by these concepts when I first heard about them. It was from John I first heard of the microcosm and the macrocosm, and what form is, and how you can "Play the room." Later, I would have students "Dance the room"—look at a window, for instance; consider a window as if it were a music score. "If that window was a dance," I'd have them say, "how many dancers impose in a dance, but the dancer and the viewer may develop another idea. After eleven years of dancing with Merce, I went to see the company for the first time as audience. Steve Paxton had taken over my roles; and watching him, I said to myself, surprised, "Oh, *that's* what I did. Oh, *that's* what that's about! Oh, *that's* what we were doing?" It was really mind-boggling. I'd thought I was doing one thing, but I saw, when I actually saw it, that it was something else.

BROWN: That philosophy was certainly prevalent in the change in painting and sculpture and art attitudes, in which the object itself, like a Mondrian, doesn't represent anything except the colors and lines. The viewer is free to associate with such a painting in any way he wishes. That philosophy was strongly influential on both Merce and John. The "thing" in itself, as Gertrude Stein said; "It-ness," "It-ness" was a matter we felt very strongly about.

SIMON: When we asked Merce to tell us more about his dancemaking process, he might answer in conundrums. Once, though, he told us that he put different movements on a chart, such as "turn head" or "lift leg" or "raise arm" or whatever; and then, using chance, he would throw pennies onto the chart to indicate combinations of these moves. But if one movement was "squat on floor" and the other was "land from a leap," we had to get from one to the other, so he would devise a transition move. That's my understanding of how some of the choreography evolved.

CHARLIP: For some of the pieces he'd make a chart of, say, possibilities for the head: "look down," "look up," "look to the right," "look to the left," "turn back," or whatever; a chart of possibilities for the arms in second, fifth, parallel; and a chart of body placements: twisting, bending, stretching. Then Merce tossed coins at the charts. He might get a head looking up while the torso was turning while the arm was moving back. But he never had us work these moves out on ourselves. He made them on himself first, then he taught them to us. So every move we made at that time was always an accepted fact.

He'd work on his own all morning, then come to class and give us these insane combinations. He'd say, "Why can't you get it?" We'd ask him to show us again, but it would be slightly different.

Merce was able to do amazing moves, where you'd be heading in one direction with your body and suddenly your leg would be whipping you around in another direction. For the dancer, the challenge was always to do completely what he'd given you, down to the last syncopation, pinky, or whatever. That was really quite difficult and kept us so busy we didn't have time to think about anything else.

BROWN: Didn't Merce always have a tendency to include a tableau, where three or four dancers would hold their positions in relationship to one another? And there was always a whirligig near the end. Chasing tails.

VAUGHAN: In the fifteen-minute stopwatch sequence that so influenced

Earle, both of you were in that rehearsal. How did you manage to get your timing so refined? It couldn't have been a conventional sense of musicality, because you weren't dancing to any sort of music, but in silence. Had you developed a kinesthetic sensitivity to some sort of rhythm that would be an alternative to traditional musical rhythm?

CHARLIP: For me it felt like being a part of a family and cooking dinner, where you get all the food ready at the same time and everybody, knowing that dinner is on the table, collects in the kitchen. Because at that point we really were a family. I lived on 7th Street and Carolyn and Earle lived on Cornelia in the Village. I'd meet Carolyn for breakfast and we'd go to Antony Tudor's or Margaret Craske's ballet class. We'd have lunch and then go to Merce's class. We'd have a rehearsal, go to dinner, and then we'd perform or go to a movie or something like that. I mean, we were with each other constantly. We began to know each other's idiosyncrasies and pleasures. We developed Marianne's version of peripheral vision. She said that in teaching children, you must develop eyes in the back of your head so that you know which kid is about to throw the paint at you.

VAUGHAN: Wouldn't you agree that even though Merce doesn't work in a conventional way with music, his choreography is intrinsically musical? The best dancers of his choreography have always been musical dancers, and Carolyn, of course, is supremely musical. It's a question of one's sense of phrasing, which doesn't have anything to do with the kind of music being played.

CHARLIP: It was also the different musicalities that we got to know. Carolyn's sense of musicality was very different from mine. As in any company, all of us argued constantly about whether we started on one foot or the other, whether a phrase faces this way or that, and so forth. Dance was our life, so we worked on music and rhythm constantly.

VAUGHAN: When did the loudness of Cunningham's music become an issue?

BROWN: At Connecticut College, the American Dance Festival. Somebody was about to sue them. A problem was that the loudspeakers would be pointing toward the audience, but David and John were behind the speakers, so they were not conscious of what was happening to the audience. If you were in line with one of those tweeters and woofers, you could get your ears knocked off.

CHARLIP: Oh, they went out into the audience, too. They heard it.

BROWN: Then it was that loud even more consciously.

CHARLIP: They wanted the sound loud. The kinds of battles that went on about it . . . I can't tell you. I remember Carolyn being very upset about the loudness of the music.

BROWN: The use of contact mikes is basic to amplification, and the first

Fragments, 1953. L to r: Merce Cunningham, Jo Anne Melsher, Marianne Preger (Simon), Carolyn Brown. Photo © Arnold Eagle.

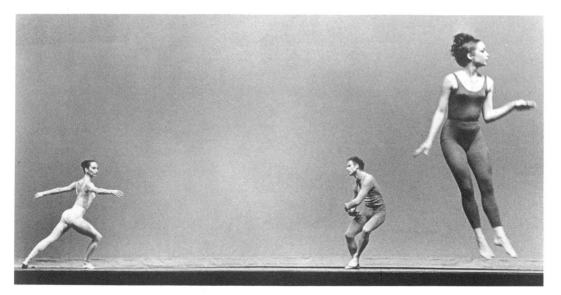

Suite for Five, 1956. L to r: Carolyn Brown, Merce Cunningham, Barbara Lloyd. Photo by Marvin Silver, courtesy Cunningham Dance Foundation.

Nocturnes, 1956. L to r: Viola Farber, Merce Cunningham, Bruce King, Marianne Preger (Simon), Carolyn Brown, Remy Charlip. Photo © Arnold Eagle.

Nocturnes. L to r: Viola Farber, Bruce King, Remy Charlip, Carolyn Brown, Merce Cunningham. Photo by Louis Stevenson, courtesy Cunningham Dance Foundation.

David Vaughan

"THEN I THOUGHT ABOUT MARCEL . . ." MERCE CUNNINGHAM'S *WALKAROUND TIME* (1982)

The practice of commissioning decors and costumes for ballet from avant-garde painters and sculptors, initiated by Sergei Diaghilev in the second period (1917–1929) of his Ballets Russes, was continued by his emulators, Rolf de Maré (Ballets Suédois) and the Comte Étienne de Beaumont (Soirées de Paris), and, less boldly, by the émigré Russian companies of the thirties and forties. It has not happened often in American ballet in the second half of the twentieth century, largely because of George Balanchine's lack of interest—some might say lack of taste—in such matters. The modern dance has a better record, notably in Merce Cunningham's long series of collaborations with some of the most advanced American painters, which parallels his equally adventurous history of musical collaboration, particularly with John Cage, which is of forty years' duration.

From 1954 to 1964, Robert Rauschenberg was the Merce Cunningham Dance Company's resident designer. In 1967 Jasper Johns became the company's artistic advisor, in which capacity he not only designed scenery and costumes himself (for *Second Hand* [1970], *Landrover* [1972], *TV Rerun* [1972], *Un Jour ou deux* [1973] for the Paris Opéra Ballet, and, later, *Exchange* [1978]) but also commissioned them from other artists: Frank Stella (*Scramble* [1967]), Andy Warhol (*RainForest* [1968]), Robert Morris (*Canfield* [1969]), Bruce Nauman (*Tread* [1970]), and Neil Jenney (*Objects* [1970]). As is well known, one of

Cunningham's major innovations is the introduction of the principle of the independence of the elements of choreography, sound, and design, as opposed to that of integration, which characterized Diaghilev's productions. These elements are created separately and brought together only in the final stages, sometimes not until the first performance.

One of the few occasions in which Cunningham diverged from this principle was in *Walkaround Time* (1968), in which the collaboration, at one remove, was with Marcel Duchamp. In the late forties and early fifties, Cunningham and Cage were friendly with members of the New York School of painters (Willem and Elaine de Kooning designed the scenery for the production of Erik Satie's play *The Ruse of Medusa* at Black Mountain College in the summer of 1948, in which Cage and Cunningham were involved). It is often suggested that Cunningham's decentralization of the stage space, largely Zen-inspired, has much in common with the way painters like Jackson Pollock handled the area of the canvas. But there was an essential difference between what Cunningham and Cage were doing and the work of the Abstract Expressionists, whose subject, as Calvin Tomkins has said, was still "the heroically suffering artist."[1] This kind of content was of course precisely what Cunningham wished to eliminate from his choreography and Cage from his music (hence their involvement with chance processes). In this they were closer to Duchamp. Like him, they wished to erase the distinction between art and life. Just as Duchamp's "ready-mades" converted everyday objects into works of art by virtue of his having chosen them, so Cunningham used non-dance movement as an element in his choreography and Cage "admitted into the purview of music the sounds, and even noises, that are part of ordinary life."[2]

Although John Cage had met Duchamp as early as 1942, it was not until the mid-1960s that he and Cunningham became close friends of Duchamp and his wife Teeny, by which time Duchamp himself had long since "retired" from active involvement with art. It was largely through Cage's transmission of his ideas that Duchamp continued to be an influence on a younger generation of artists. A Duchamp collaboration with the Merce Cunningham Dance Company, however desirable, was unlikely. As Cunningham tells it, the genesis of *Walkaround Time* was casual, spontaneous:

> We were at dinner at Duchamp's apartment on 10th Street, John and Teeny were playing chess, and I was sitting there with Lois [Long] and Jasper [Johns], and Marcel was over there smoking a pipe, watching the chess game—he didn't have to watch, he knew what was going on without looking. And Jasper said to me, would you be interested in doing something with *The Large Glass*? And I said, oh yes—just automatically. So he said, then I'll ask Marcel. And he went over, and they talked and he came back and I said, what did he say? And Jasper said, well, he looked pained—he asked who would do all the work. And Jasper had said, I would, and Marcel said, oh, fine.
>
> That was the way that began. The only thing that Marcel asked was

that at some point it be assembled to look like the *Glass* as much as possible, and that's what happens at the end. Jasper figured out how to divide it, I'm sure he talked with Marcel—he had the idea of silk-screening [the images] on to some kind of transparent material. I think they had to do it twice—either the silk-screening wouldn't take, or it wouldn't stand up, or whatever. They wanted to do it with helium in it, like the [*RainForest*] pillows, but that wouldn't work. So it ended up with this idea of their being inflated: five of them standing and two hung.

Then I thought about Marcel. . . .[3]

Walkaround Time, then, differs from other Cunningham works in that all the elements are related to the central idea of a kind of *hommage à Duchamp.* The decor, as indicated, is an adaptation of Duchamp's magnum opus, whose full title is *The Bride Stripped Bare by Her Bachelors, Even,* supervised by Johns. The music is not by Cage but by David Behrman; its title, *. . . for nearly an hour. . .,* refers not only to the actual duration of the dance but to another Duchamp work related to the *Glass, To be looked at (from the other side of the glass) with one eye, close to, for nearly an hour* (1918). (Cunningham's own title for the dance comes not from a Duchamp work but from computer jargon: it refers to the time when the computer is running and the programmer can "walk around" until it is finished. At the end of the dance, when the seven inflatables have been assembled in an approximation of the original, the dancers do in fact walk around in a circle behind them, then sit.)

It is not surprising that Cunningham's choreography pays homage to various aspects of Duchamp's work in general rather than finding some kind of dance equivalent of the specific, erotic content of the *Glass* itself; such content is rarely to be found in his dances and in any case such a literal approach is alien to his method. Although he has said, "I put in lots of things about Duchamp and his work," he added, "I never tell anybody because this confuses people."[4]

The main thing, I think, is the tempo. Marcel always gave one the sense of a human being who is ever calm, a person with an extraordinary sense of calmness, as though days could go by, and minutes could go by. And I wanted to see if I could get that—the sense of time.[5]

Walkaround Time begins with the dancers disposed about the stage, surrounded by the decor. There is a long moment of stillness, and then they slowly begin to do various movements that anyone familiar with Cunningham technique will recognize as the opening warm-up exercises of his class (back stretches, knee bends). Cunningham customarily works out passages of choreography in his classes, and then develops them further in rehearsal, usually in the direction of greater complication, but here the exercises are transferred to the stage almost without alteration; hence, this is one form of choreographic "ready-made." Another may be found in the repetition in the second half of sequences of movement from the first half of the dance (Cunningham was pleased when he heard that a small boy in the audience at the first performance had said, "Look, they're doing reruns").

Cunningham does not, as might have been expected, use everyday movement as an element in the choreography of the dance proper, but in between the two parts there is an intermission, when the house lights are brought up and the dancers stroll onto the stage wearing bathrobes and do the kind of thing they would ordinarily do during an intermission with the curtain down—sit and chat, practice steps, lie down. Behrman's sound score gives way to recordings of popular music (Argentine tangos, a Japanese soprano singing *Tristesse*). All these, of course, are ready-mades in yet another sense.

The intermission also refers to the cinematic *Entr'acte* (by René Clair) from the Dadaist ballet *Relâche*, presented by the Ballets Suédois in 1924, with music by Satie and decor, costumes, and scenario by Francis Picabia, in which Duchamp himself appeared. In the ballet, he appeared almost naked, as Adam in a *tableau vivant* after Lucas Cranach; in the film, he is seen playing chess with Man Ray.[6]

Finally, the moment when one of the male dancers (originally Gus Solomons jr) is picked up and carried across the stage by the others, is interpreted by Cunningham as follows: "You have an object—or a person if you like—and then that object is transported and you see it, or him, in another circumstance—he's the same, but the situation has changed."[7]

Shortly after the end of the *entr'acte*, Cunningham enters, stands behind one of the set pieces, and while running in place peels off one set of leotard and tights and pulls on another. Both the striptease and the repetition of movement while it is performed refer to Duchamp's *Nude Descending a Staircase*. Cunningham also tried to convey the sense of "stopping and moving at the same time" that characterizes the *Nude* in Carolyn Brown's solo, where stillness alternates with fast, large movement.[8]

Cunningham describes going into the studio and asking "one of the dancers to do a back fall . . .; then I asked one of the men to fall over her, and I asked another girl to fall over them."[9] It is possible to discern in the resulting convoluted figure (which recurs several times, at different tempi, during the piece) a reference to the machinelike images of *The Large Glass* itself. Again, at various moments, particularly at the end, when the decor is assembled in an approximation of the original (Duchamp's only stipulation), the dancers are seen behind the set pieces, and we are reminded of an important aspect of the *Glass*—that the images are not only to be looked at, but seen through.

Charles Atlas, director of the film version of *Walkaround Time* (1973), suggests a further correlation with this aspect of the work:

> Cunningham has translated Duchamp's concern with transparency in terms of movements into a dance composition which explores the possibilities of lateral movements back and forth across a proscenium space. In addition to the "transparent" clarity of this way of shaping space (as against, for example, the use of a swirling space) this is movement that

and sequence of the sounds will be. In some dances, sections of the choreography are shifted around from performance to performance, so that there can be no set narrative or dramatic line. Cunningham's dancers don't attempt to relate to the decor in which they move, except in the most practical sense. When Andy Warhol's gently floating silver pillows get in their way in *Rain-Forest* they plow right through them. Or the visual imagery may change drastically from one performance to the next, as in *Scramble*, where Frank Stella's brightly colored rectangles of cloth stretched at different levels on aluminum frames are moved around so that whole sections of the dance might be invisible to some of the audience. In *Variations V* (1965), six projectors throw a cacophony of moving and still images onto the stage, but the dancers act as if nothing were happening. (Compare this with Robert Joffrey's popular but conventional mixed-media ballet *Astarte*, in which the music and the film/ lighting sequence begin together and are precisely timed to coincide with and complement the dancing.)

Never to my knowledge has Merce Cunningham given an "interpretation" of any of his dances, nor do any of his associates. They will talk about the movement, what it is like, how it was made, what chance operations were used in putting it together, but they won't divulge the message or even the mood, as if it wasn't their business to be concerned with those things. Since I have no reason to believe that Cunningham and his people are either so naîve as to be unaware that they are always creating some kind of theater event, or so cagey as to pretend that they are not, I can only assume that they are deliberately maintaining their neutrality. There is in their attitude a certain fatalistic cheerfulness; they intend to do their job no matter what goes on around them. If every member of the audience has a different idea of what they're doing, or if the stage environment changes, still the integrity of their own task is constant. You can imagine them completing their appointed rounds in the dark, or if a dancer were injured or the theater were in flames.

Nevertheless, a Cunningham dance *is* a theatrical entity, especially in contrast to the work of some younger choreographers who have distilled his theories into more austere and concentrated forms. Judith Dunn uses nonsequential movement, Yvonne Rainer stresses the simultaneous, antiemotional quality of events, and Twyla Tharp turns chance operations into mathematical monotony. None of these choreographers uses other theater elements to the extent Cunningham does, and where their work seems cold and abstract, his takes on a dramatic life that he apparently neither dictates nor denies. The audience does have to find its own specific metaphors and relationships, but each piece usually has an overall sensibility that is apparent to everyone.

For me, Cunningham's dark pieces have suggested more specific "meanings" than his brighter works. The latter, which include *Field Dances* (1963), *Scramble* (1967), *Walkaround Time* (1968), and others, are expansive, flooded with light and color, pervaded with a general air of good fellowship and the joy of movement. In the dark pieces, the lighting and colors are somber, the movement is more restricted, the dancers seem more isolated from each other and at the same time more submissive to their environment. I feel in these works, especially *Winterbranch* (1964), *Place* (1966), *RainForest* (1968), and now *Canfield* (1969), that Cunningham is responding—perhaps unconsciously—to the ugly demands of civilization, rather than ignoring them.

There seems to be a progression from *Winterbranch*, where the dancers are crushed by merciless light and total darkness and a maniacally screeching sound track; to *Place*, where they rush frantically at the boundaries of some nameless enclosure and finally break out of it into some other unknown darkness; through *RainForest*, where they seem poised between their human-ness and some nonhuman existence that could be either animalistic or artifi-cial, and that they cannot attain in any case. Now, in *Canfield*, the dancers seem to have become resigned to a bland, computerized state in which both the joy and the rebellion have been diminished to faint emotions that can be easily countermanded by the more powerful hand of technology.

The dancers are in gray leotards against a white cyclorama and ungelled lights. The legs and borders masking the perimeter of the stage have been flown out; the space is enormous and the dancers look insignificant in it. A huge vertical boom travels constantly back and forth across the proscenium, with lights inside it, projecting onto the cyc. Sometimes the dancers are pinned in its glare, like escaping convicts in a searchlight; sometimes they drift in the gloom beyond its reach.

The movement seemed pale, the dynamics easy, without much thrust or conviction. There was rather more unison movement than in the average Cunningham dance, and an occasional theme of brushing past each other, making contact at the shoulder but without enough impact to upset each other's direction or momentum. Toward the end a huge bare leko bulb is projected on the cyc, then an indistinct man's face, then the lights in the boom begin to fade, looking somehow not like stage lights dimming but like the brown fatality of a power failure—and the curtain comes down on moving gray ciphers.

But it is the sound that dominates *Canfield*, a sound devised by Pauline Oliveros (*In Memoriam: Nikola Tesla, Cosmic Engineer*) that by its literalness and its overriding force insistently calls attention to itself in an unequal competition with what is going on on the stage.

Ever since Merce Cunningham began choreographing in 1942, his musical activities have been directed by John Cage. The two work amiably yet quite independently together. Each pursues his own inventions; the moment of collaboration is the moment of performance; and it is either a recurring accident or a figment of the critic's orderly mind that the two disparate parts seem so frequently to be in consonance with each other. Cunningham seems to have no egotistical notions about the dance being more important than the know that extreme noise can reduce or otherwise alter your perceptual powers. But even when it is not physically uncomfortable, the *Canfield* sound is literal, which can be even more distracting. What is it about words that makes us pay attention to them? There are ways of de-emphasizing a verbal dance accompaniment, as Cunningham does in *How to Pass, Kick, Fall and Run* (1965), where Cage and David Vaughan read low-key selections from Cage's writings, sometimes overlapping each other. Then we can choose to listen to one or the other, or to neither, letting their combined flow of words make an abstract background for the dance. But in *Canfield* the drama behind those banal dialogues is inescapable. How *could* I be interested in those efficient, faceless men with their dreary talk of inputs and readings? But I am, I'm fascinated, I strain to make out the words when the tuning drifts away. I hate myself and I hate the sound, because I'm missing the dance.

Well, maybe this *is* the dance.

A few days after the Brooklyn Academy season, *The New York Times* reported that an eminent biologist told Senator Edmund Muskie's committee investigating pollution that "in the process of creating new goods and services, technology is destroying the country's 'capital' of land, water, and other resources as well as injuring people." In fact, scarcely a day goes by that we are not offered pronouncements, pamphlets, threats, warnings, and predictions of disaster resulting from the masochistic and perhaps irreversible course of technological exploitation. Intentionally or not, Merce Cunningham is going beyond the tracts and the vague dread. He is showing us postmillennial man—wired for sound, dissolving into his colorless backdrop, ineffectually and without regrets, alive. The image is more vivid and more terrifying than all the dead fish in the Hudson and all the polemics in Congress. And our response is to cover our ears, as Merce Cunningham, wise as a stone, probably always knew we would.

*   *   *   *

Some time after this article was written, the astronauts landed on the moon. After watching their televised performance, Merce Cunningham's manager, Jean Rigg, told Merce Cunningham that the lighting effects on the moon were exactly what they had been trying for in *Canfield*. Merce Cunningham said, "Yes! And the sound too."

Stephen Smoliar

MERCE CUNNINGHAM IN BROOKLYN (1970)

I want to write about Merce Cunningham and the concerts given by his company at the Brooklyn Academy of Music during the month of January 1970. I suppose this means I want to write about dance, but it's not just a matter of writing about dance—even though in most cases, dance, music, and set are independent elements. It's a matter of writing about environments—however overburdened the literature of art criticism may be with that word already.

But that's all right. I've always regarded Merce Cunningham as being involved in more than just the art of making dances. He is an architect of the theater, building (in cooperation with musicians and artists) an entire world for his audiences—be it on a proscenium stage such as the one at the Brooklyn Academy or in a gymnasium or museum. I do not go to Cunningham's concerts simply for dance; I go for a total theatrical experience. This entails quite a universe, and many audiences are inclined to think it is more than they can handle. But one doesn't "handle" Cunningham's productions; one simply has to observe them. The rest is totally within the mind of the observer, who may direct his attention wherever he desires at any time and fashion his own personal experience. So in writing about Merce Cunningham's concerts, I am simply recording my own experiences—hence, the reason for this diary format.

The season began with *Canfield* (1969); and *Canfield* began with Pauline Oliveros's *In Memoriam: Nikola Tesla, Cosmic Engineer*, which started as the house lights were dimming. In an amplified conversation conducted from the

77

tape recordings from a realization he had already prepared on Richard Lippold's Schlicker baroque organ—a two-person realization accomplished by overdubbing.

From a purely subjective point of view, *Tread* was very enjoyable—even fun. One could safely call it refreshing, with all those fans blowing on the audience; but the beautiful thing about it all was the comfortable, relaxed attitude of the dancers throughout the piece. Some of the interactions involved strange and awkward contortions, but you never felt afraid to laugh at something that looked silly. The dancers themselves were quite prone to cracking smiles and the general atmosphere was one of—if you will pardon the expression—an antic meet.

Tread was followed by another cheerful piece—*How to Pass, Kick, Fall and Run* (1965). Here the movements were strictly physical—intentionally devoid of any of the tedious overtones too often associated with modern dance. The accompaniment consisted of an ensemble of stories by John Cage, read by Cage and David Vaughan, sometimes reading different stories simultaneously.

This type of accompaniment brought out a problem also present in *Canfield*—the dominating effect of the human voice. The Cage stories and the amplified discussion among the musicians had a tremendous command of the attention—enough to distract it from the stage. Perhaps the problem has to do with a subconscious desire for meaning which can be satisfied—at least superficially—by language.

I already mentioned my difficulties in trying to keep track of the choreography of *Canfield*. *How to* is a much more relaxed affair, and I never really feel I *have* to pay attention to anything. Things just seem to take care of themselves. It is impossible to mistake the generally bouncy atmosphere of the dance no matter how assiduously one follows the stories. *How to Pass, Kick, Fall and Run* can be taken strictly for fun—whether it comes from the stories, the dance, or a combination of the two.

*   *   *   *

Scramble (1967) is one of the hardest dances for me to discuss intelligently. It may be because the work is what Gus Solomons jr. called "a real *dance* dance," and one can only grab a handle on it in terms of dance—that is, a fluent articulation of movement. If one is a dancer, particularly if one is well-trained in Cunningham's technique, this is not particularly difficult. Otherwise, *Scramble* is a work which demands several viewings. The bulk of Calvin Tomkins's *New Yorker* essay on Cunningham is about the making of *Scramble*; and I would like to quote two excerpts which describe the piece straight out:

> *Scramble* was certainly not indeterminate, nor did chance play much of a role in its creation. Cunningham kept experimenting with the order of its various parts. By the middle of June, he had blocked out three main sections of the dance. There would be four sections in all, and his idea was

that each one would be complete in itself. The longest section was the one that began with the whole company running four times across the stage. The fourth time across, Sandra Neels and Gus Solomons (whose part is now danced by Jeff Slayton) fell to the floor and remained there while the others went off; then, rising slowly, they began a sinuous, erotic duet, which led into Sandra's solo. This section also included the Carolyn Brown solo with the swimming movement and a Brown-Cunningham duet, which began with her taking extended positions while he scrambled (literally) under her outstretched arm or leg. The duet then erupted into a very active series of rapid leaps and pirouettes, criss-crossing the stage and ending when she made a startling head-first leap into the wings, where she was caught by Gus Solomons and Albert Reid (now Chase Robinson) . . . *Scramble* would begin with the section that the dancers had learned most recently, in which they came in slowly, one by one, from the wings, each with a different sort of sinuous movement, until they formed a tight group at the center of the stage. Cunningham then sprang into the quirky, complex phrase that had given Barbara Lloyd trouble earlier, and, one by one, they followed him until all of them were dancing the phrase in unison. This was followed by a new Cunningham solo, which the dancers now saw for the first time. The solo progressed through odd crouchings and twistings of the body to a passage in which Cunningham seemed to be making karate motions with his arms (he had seen an exhibition of karate and judo at Town Hall in the spring, and it fascinated him), and then he began a loose, loping, circling movement about the stage. As he was finishing the circling movement one day, he suddenly shouted—an angry roar that sounded more animal than human. The dancers thought for a moment that he had hurt himself. When he continued to dance, unperturbed, they realized that it must be part of the solo.

A few remarks by Cunningham on *Scramble* are also relevant to the performance: "The order of things can be changed, the timing. We can stop and start at any point. I've kept it that way on purpose. . . . It's taking its own shape and life, from now on my job is to avoid interfering with it . . . we can move the sets . . . oh, yes, it's going to work . . . have a good time."

Scramble is built about the ambiguities of its title—the physical action of scrambling about, the military jargon of scrambling a code, scrambling eggs. And the fact that the ordering of the dance was not fixed is yet another realization of the concept—this particular performance was a scrambling of the version described by Tomkins.

Between phonograph records and movies, we have been accustomed to believing that consistency of title implies consistency of contents. This is the first step on the road to the death of the live performing arts. The important thing about *Scramble* is that while two performances may not look exactly alike, they both look like *Scramble*. The question then, as far as this particular performance is concerned, is how did *Scramble* feel? Cunningham writes that the timing may be changed, and the timing of this performance was one which ever seen *Crises*—although I had read much about it—and consequently, I saw many things in the second viewing which I had missed the first time around. For example, at first glance one notices that Viola Farber's costume is yellow while all the others are red. However, this is not so simple, because the red costumes range over a continuum of hues—from the dark, bold red of Cunningham's costume to Carolyn Brown's pale pink. In this context, the color of Miss Farber's costume takes on another interpretation. Not only is it a different color; but within this continuum, it is a color which is "falling off the brink" of the fading sequence of reds. This wording is particularly appropriate in terms of the qualities of her movement. The various quiverings of her body—particularly when they occur simultaneously with a long, steady extension—convey the impression of one on the edge of insanity. (As a matter of fact, there has been a fair amount of research in the matter of how body movements reflect a person's mental condition.) *Crises* is a downright terrifying experience. Not just because Miss Farber seems to be "falling off the brink," but because everyone else gives off that same hint. When Susana Hayman-Chaffey assists her in her jumps, Miss Farber appears helplessly dependent on everyone else. But when the other girls (there are four in the cast) start trembling the same way she does, or when they project those long, intense stares with ghostly empty eyes, it's as if the whole world was mad and she was the only one with even the faintest comprehension of sanity.

The third time around, *Tread* looked like it was being performed the third time around. The sparkle was missing, the house was very empty, and the audience seemed quite stolid. One sympathizes with the dampened spirits on stage. Tomorrow night they won't perform *Tread* and that's good. The piece needs a rest.

* * * *

Walkaround Time (1968) serves as a fine introduction to Merce Cunningham and—for that matter—to the modern dance experience. The initial sequences of body stretches executed by the company are drawn straight from Cunningham's technique classes, and many of the combinations that follow could also have easily evolved from those classes. This is not to imply that the piece is elementary or simplistic. Quite the contrary—it's "what it's all about." It takes a series of movement structures which are so familiar to many dance students that they execute them without thinking, and places them in the context of dance—thus forcing one to think about them again. These exercises and combinations now become atoms of energy in the vast molecular structure which *Walkaround Time* envelops.

The title apparently comes from the computer jargon at the University of Illinois. It refers to that period of time during which the computer is running a program. In most circles this is referred to as "run time"; but of course that is from the computer's point of view. As far as the programmers are concerned, "walkaround time" is an appropriate expression.

The dance itself actually has such a period of walkaround time—that is, a period of waiting for something to happen before one can proceed. Halfway through the piece, the house lights come up; and although the curtain never descends, it is quite obvious that this is a period of intermission. At this particular performance most of the dancers just lay around in leg warmers. Mel Wong was doing exercises, and Meg Harper and Valda Setterfield were teaching some new steps to Douglas Dunn. The important thing about this episode is that it was totally informal—unstructured and spontaneous.

However, this provided a way of looking at the structured sections on either side of this intermission. The work was a carefully assembled montage of those activities which may be encountered during walkaround time— exercises, combinations for practice (in one series of leaps, Carolyn Brown looked away from the audience at Jeff Slayton, as if they were still practicing the alignment), and even idle recreation. Near the end of the dance, there was a period of work, as the dancers moved Jasper John's large plastic cubes based on the components of Marcel Duchamp's *The Large Glass* to the back of the stage. (The more ambitious computer programmers work on other problems during walkaround time.) Once this wall had been constructed, the dancers walked around behind it, and then sat down as the curtain descended.

The following background information was provided for *Second Hand*, the second new work of this season:

> In 1944 Merce Cunningham made *Idyllic Song*, using an arrangement for two pianos by John Cage of the first movement of Erik Satie's *Socrate*, a work for orchestra and voices having three movements: The Banquet; On the Banks of the Illysus; Death of Socrates. In the summer of 1969 Cunningham approached the work again with the plan to complete it. The two-piano arrangement by Cage was finished in October 1969 in collaboration with Arthur Maddox. Permission for the use of this arrangement was not granted by the copyright holder. The use of Satie's own arrangement for voices and piano solo was also not permitted. Cage, using *I Ching* chance operations with respect to seven modes and twelve transpositions of each, and applying these in a programmed way to his model, made a new composition preserving the rhythm and expressivity of the original.

Second Hand (1970) was totally unlike anything yet presented in the season. The only thing I can relate it to would be *Suite for Five* (1956), but it was even calmer and more placid than that. The first part remained an extensive solo by Cunningham, the second, a duet with Carolyn Brown. Only the final section involved the entire company. John Cage's music—a piano solo called *Cheap Imitation*—was soft, slow, and almost entirely monophonic. It was a true homage to Satie with all the purity of his simplicity, although the *I Ching* chance operations yielded melodic lines quite reminiscent of certain computer-composed melodies I have heard.

The dance itself does appear to be second-hand in a most remarkable way.

to that sort of imagination. The sporadic behavior of light in the midst of a general darkness and the sense of defeatism embodied in the action of falling both lend suggestions of a tremendous disaster to *Winterbranch*. The lighting makes it like a ride through a spooky funhouse. You are allowed only momentary glimpses as you are hurtled through a maze of terrors.

Is it worth mentioning the ill behavior of the audience? Was I naive enough to believe such things didn't happen in New York? Or is Brooklyn really that different from New York? Most of the dissidents were adequately put down by the accompaniment, La Monte Young's *2 Sounds (April 1960)*. It simply blasted the hell out of them and wouldn't let them complain. In fact, the tape ended early; and the entire audience heaved a collective sigh of relief in the final moments of silence. However, the enormous ovation at the end of *Winterbranch* best reflected the opinion of the heretofore "silent majority." After six years, *Winterbranch* still seems to pack the strongest punch.

*   *   *   *

With two days of rest, *Tread* returned—again cheerful and bouncy. There are so many precious moments in this piece! Sandra Neels's bursting energy as she climbs all over Jeff Slayton in their duet. The bemused look on Valda Setterfield's face as she is carried off on Chase Robinson's shoulder. And Meg Harper struggling to crawl through the fragment of space under Jeff Slayton's leg. *Tread* is not a string of gags. It is almost deadly for the dancers. Nonetheless, it is a highly amusing situation. It is curious that a piece like *Winterbranch*, whose movements are fundamentally simple, just seems to reek of disaster, while *Tread*, which is in reality a more dangerous work, can shine with a cheery disposition.

Like *RainForest*, *Place* (1966) leaves much to the imagination. However, while *RainForest* is essentially animal in effect, the implicit atmosphere of *Place* is more mechanical. Gordon Mumma's *Mesa*, which accompanies the dance, is as reminiscent of some surrealistic factory as *RainForest* is of the jungle. The sounds dig into the environment with the strength and determination of a buzz saw attacking a plank of wood.

Within this sonic context, the dance also takes on machine-like qualities. There are ensemble sections in which each dancer executes a periodic activity of different length, giving the overall appearance of some unworldly juggernaut constructed of human bodies. Furthermore, their faces are so expressionless that the effect is of a soulless, demonic machine—particularly when juxtaposed with Cunningham's contrastingly expressive solos. As in *Winterbranch*, where the feeling is also not explicit, there is a desperate sense of futility in *Place* which reaches a heartbreaking climax with Cunningham struggling within a plastic bag.

Once again, I was in a trance when *Second Hand* was all over. It is an unusual work for Cunningham in many respects. For instance, it was clearly choreographed to music; and this factor was so important that Cage was extremely careful to preserve the phrase structures of the intended accompaniment, *Socrate*, in his own *Cheap Imitation*. Also, the dance does not appear to be as seminal as other pieces. Rather than proceeding as a sequence of disjunct episodes, it appears to have a well-woven contrapuntal fabric which yields the sort of internal coherence one might expect from more classical works. Is not, then, *Second Hand* a reactionary phase within the context of Cunningham's innovations? I don't think so, because many of the ideas of these innovations are still being developed. Cunningham once wrote of one of his early solos: "The dance as performed seems to have an unmistakable dramatic intensity in its bones, so to speak. It seems to me that it is simply a question of allowing this quality to happen rather than of forcing it." Such is the case for *Second Hand*.

* * * *

Tonight *Walkaround Time* seemed to break down into three basic types of episodes. There were those sections which may be traced back to combinations from technique classes. There were the complex group constructions which have some of the same structural qualities as *Place*. Finally, there were the "walkaround" episodes which held the piece together.

In this respect, *Walkaround Time* was a dance about dancers. This was most evident during the intermission where the dancers were most free to be themselves. It was one of those exciting little "behind the scenes" glimpses of artists as they are "in real life." And the remarkable thing about *Walkaround Time* is that the Cunningham dancers were good about being natural when they were put on the spot in this manner.

Concerning the excerpts from technique classes—these were, of course, the building blocks of the entire dance. The work began, logically enough, with stillness; then it proceeded to the first set of exercises—a warmup, if you will. Finally, it progressed into the more complex constructions which we are inclined to call "real dance" (if there is such a thing). At the very end of the piece, the dancers went back to simply walking around and eventually sat down and came to rest.

The dance does go on "for nearly an hour" (the title of David Behrman's accompanying score), but a skillful articulation of the individual episodes does not make it seem overly long. The intermission is particularly valuable in this respect, and there is no real reason why the audience shouldn't be as free to "walk around" as are the dancers. After all, intermissions belong to everybody.

The music for *Scramble*—Toshi Ichiyanagi's *Activities for Orchestra*—had more of that sense of a continuum which I found lacking at the last performance; but the dance still seemed to have an isolated quality. That feeling of a pervading energy which drives the company—both individually and in groups—was missing. This may be due to a certain amount of fatigue on the part of the company. After all, every dancer has to perform every night. On the other hand, it may be due to fatigue on the part of the critic. It took tremendous

Richard Kostelanetz

CUNNINGHAM'S SELF-BOOK (1969)

Among the more valuable traditions established in the late sixties was the practice of consequential vanguard artists creating imaginatively designed books primarily about their own work and esthetic position—not only Allan Kaprow and Claes Oldenberg, but Andy Warhol's *Index* (1967), Iain Baxter's *A Portfolio of Piles* (1968), Dick Higgins' *foew&ombwhnw* (1969), and John Cage's *Notations* (1969), among others. (The last book, by accepting within its own frame everything offered by selected other composers, is perhaps aesthetically more self-appropriate than Cage's two collections of essays, despite the patent compromise, in *Notations,* of such an unenhancing convention as presenting the contributions in alphabetical order.) Merce Cunningham's *Changes: Notes on Choreography* (1969) resembles its predecessors in the crucial aspect of being as much *like* as about Cunningham's dance.

The inside front cover has overlapping lines of crossing type on top of a photograph, a form reminiscent of the beams of light passing over dancers in *Winterbranch* (1964); a page in the middle has a column of type running down the center, superimposed over both a photograph and the program of *Variations V* (1965), very much like the disconnected simultaneity of the piece itself; and the structure of the entire book is as concentrated in discrete detail (the page) but as plotless and non-climactic in overall form as Cunningham's choreography. While materials relevant to a particular piece are generally grouped together, the fragments are not presented in chronological order, the author avoiding one compromise of convenience; and need one say that this is not the sort of self-book that either George Balanchine or Martha Graham would publish.

Just as Cunningham's *Walkaround Time* (1968) freely mixes movement, sound, stillness, and lights and decor, so *Changes* mixes with similar freedom shrewdly chosen photographs, reproductions of performance programs and handwritten notes, rough sketches and diagrams, neatly typed remarks that were apparently transcribed recently (on the same multiple-font machine that Cage favors); letters written to friends, scribbled replies to a questionnaire, aesthetic declarations, etc., etc. ("Dancing has a continuity of its own that need not be dependent on either the rise or fall of sound, or the pitch and cry of words. Its force of feeling lies in the physical image, fleeting or static.") Contained within this unpaginated potpourri are also some edifying descriptions of how chance procedures can be adapted to the gamut of choreographic variables.

In general, the pieces strike this nondancer (but sometime football player) as thoughtfully and thoroughly planned, even in their allowances for various degrees and kinds of indeterminacy (as in professional football—one hears, Cunningham's favorite spectator sport). Only an artist as unpretentious, unevasive, and succinct in his prose as Cunningham would admit, on one hand, that a 1944 dance, *Root of an Unfocus,* "was concerned with fear," or that in a more recent aleatory work "I find No. 9 and No. 10 were not used, did not come up as possibilities; and upon examining them carefully, I am relieved they did not." (The obvious point lost in the shuffling discussion is that while chance methods have the virtue of producing results beyond the conventions of premeditated choreography, not everything aleatory would be equally successful.)

"Dancing is movement in time and space," he announces early in *Changes,* and a book, by analogy, is filled pages between the frame of covers. Populating this canvas is the achievement of the writer and designer Frances Starr, who brilliantly adapted Cunningham's compositonal syntax to the bookish medium (that, need one add, more desperately requires stylistic resuscitation than, say, the ballet). It is true that texts printed upside-down provide a bit of a nuisance, while in the middle of the book is reproduced a program whose year-date is perversely blocked out or omitted despite Cunningham's handwritten inscription, "I date my beginnings from this concert." Nonetheless, scattered between the covers is much genuine information and explanation unavailable elsewhere.

This book-composition is also a highly contemporary way for an artist-still-in-progress to forge a permanent but incomplete record of his own career. However, since this volume eschews an explanatory preface or recapitulatory afterword, the reader is left the task of interpreting significances from the evidence presented. He who does not comprehend Cunningham's choreographic imagination is not likely to understand this book, for *Changes* demands the sort of perceptual procedures honed on Cunningham's dance, not to speak of Cage's music and perhaps William Burroughs's fictions, too.

These figures and dates in themselves attest to Cunningham's interest in Events.

One's first Event, if bewildering, may also be fun. It's a lark—"something different." But as Event follows Event, bewilderment may turn to dismay as it dawns upon one that Events, far from being regarded as mere novelties, have been legitimized as major endeavors by the Cunningham company. Moreover, they raise fearful questions, not only about the nature of Cunningham's art, but about art in general. The kinds of questions they invite are those implicit in the shocked exclamation of a friend a few years ago after attending some Cunningham Events: "He's dismantling his repertoire!"

As is often true of developments in the performing arts, Cunningham's current predilections may involve practicality as well as pure esthetics. By mixing older works together, Cunningham may keep much of his repertoire active. Simultaneously, he can try out new composers and designers. The flexibility of the Event format makes it possible to adapt his choreography to each fresh performing situation he encounters: Events fit easily into studios, gyms, museums, and lofts, as well as into conventional theaters. Yet, ultimately, these are Cunningham's concerns, not those of the audience. Audiences always want a "good show." If a certain performance procedure cannot produce one, then it should be scrapped, no matter how otherwise practical it is. Thus, we are led from practical to esthetic difficulties. And, to some dancegoers, they seem enormous.

Still, Events should not have prompted quite the amount of shocked surprise that they did, since they can be interpreted as logical outgrowths of basic Cunningham theories. Cunningham has always been fascinated by fluid performing situations, by live theater as something inherently unfixed. In dance of any kind, even when choreography is scrupulously set, no two performances will ever be exactly the same because of the cast's differing physical and mental conditions at each of those performances. To go to the theater is always chancy. Cunningham has long capitalized upon theater's uncertainties. For instance, he has created dances consisting of several parts which can be performed in any number of possible orders. Similarly, the music and decor for his pieces occupy the same space and time as the dance but usually do not imitate or logically relate to anything in the choreography—a practice which makes Cunningham simultaneously a Diaghilevian and a non-Diaghilevian choreographer: Diaghilevian because he commissions composers and painters, non-Diaghilevian because he makes no effort to have all parts of a production lock tightly together like pieces of a jigsaw puzzle. Once the parts of a single piece are regarded as potentially interchangeable, one is only a short step of the imagination away from thinking that all parts of all one's pieces are similarly interchangeable, and when that step is taken the Event is born. But some audiences may wonder whether that step ought to be taken. Has Cunningham this time really gone too far?

Unquestionably, the Events intimidate. To begin with, there is often nothing—or very little—that one can say about them. We are such verbal creatures that not being able to come up with a well-organized verbal assessment of our perceptions can be frustrating. No wonder a few critics are particularly annoyed by Events, for critics are by necessity the most verbal dancegoers of all. But what is there to say about an Event?

Well, one could try to describe it. Most Events are open in form, but some exhibit simple structural characteristics which may be noted. Thus, one recent Event was, whether by forethought or happenstance, constructed according to a pattern which Louis Horst, after gnashing his teeth, might have classified as extended ABAB or rondo form: a group section was followed by a solo which was followed by another group, and so on. One could continue trying to say something about an Event by recording in exact detail each action as it occurred. If one possessed the necessary skills, one could even notate it.

But what really would be accomplished by that? For there might still exist an inexplicable gap between the actions themselves and one's responses of delight, horror, or befuddlement. At least, Cunningham's individual dance works, though abstract, do seem to be "about" something, because each establishes an atmosphere or emphasizes some quality of movement so that, say, *Summerspace* (1958) looks genuinely distinct from *Winterbranch* (1964). The Events, however, remain impregnable. There they are: great hunks of theater, seemingly unapproachable.

There is, though, at least one way of regarding Events which can make them less forbidding, a point of view emanating from the philosophy which produced them in the first place. Cunningham, John Cage, and other artists in their circle regard art as an imitation of nature—but not in any literal sense, for that might result in nothing more than a superfluous replication of objects. Rather, they wish to imitate nature in its manner of operation. For them, the universe is Heraclitean, forever open to metamorphoses. Events, then, are attempts to reproduce in miniature the workings of the universe. In Events things happen and are transformed into other things happening, images are born and disintegrate and reshape themselves into other images. Everything has its own form, yet form is always subject to modification. Frequently, even when the choreography is vigorous, Events somehow possess an overall feeling of imperturbability or even serenity. They resemble such phenomena as the running of rivers, the formation of crystals, the orbits of planets, or the flow of traffic through the streets: they partake of some process which can be related to the basic processes of earthly existence. The "experience of dance" which Cunningham says he desires Events to provide is thus very much like the experience of life itself.

Even the length of Events is significant. Ninety minutes, uninterrupted, is a sizable chunk of choreographic time. It is long enough to seem an eternity. It is also long enough to prevent one from thinking in terms of beginning, has established a dialogue between everything and something. He not only provides us with different kinds of things to see, he reminds us that the same things may be seen in different ways. The pieces isolate and frame, the Events are all-inclusive. If we want to, if we need to, we can even put up our own frames of attention around the action in Events. Cunningham probably won't object: he gives us the freedom to make up our minds.

Carolyn Brown, Douglas Dunn, Viola Farber, Steve Paxton, Marianne Preger Simon, Valda Setterfield, Gus Solomons jr, David Vaughan

CUNNINGHAM AND HIS DANCERS (1987)

DAVID VAUGHAN: When Merce Cunningham was in his prime as a dancer, how did he work with his dancers in terms of communicating the choreographic material that made the early pieces? And as the advancing years have brought on physical limitations, how have his working methods changed—or have they? How has his choreography changed—or has it? Marianne Preger Simon was in the original company from 1953 to 1959. What can you tell us?

MARIANNE SIMON: My memory is that he gave us pieces to do for the middle of the class when there was dancing to be done, and they were usually portions of dances that he was demonstrating. That was how we learned some of them. Others he would demonstrate for us individually and teach us step by step.

VIOLA FARBER: When I first joined the Cunningham company—

VAUGHAN: Viola was in it from 1953 to 1965 and returned briefly as a guest artist in 1970.

FARBER:—Merce was working on two dances, and I don't think I knew that they had names. I never knew which dance we were learning parts of. When the point came that he said, "Let's do *Septet* (1953)," I thought, "Which steps are those?" I don't know if anyone else had that experience or if I was particularly stupid, but I do remember that. I'd no idea which dance we were working on, because we learned steps.

101

VAUGHAN: But at that time, of course, he was working on quite a large repertory, wasn't he, for the first performances of what became the Cunningham company?

FARBER: Yes. He was working on two dances.

VAUGHAN: Oh, just two? Do you remember what the other one was? I should point out that Marianne, Viola, and Carolyn Brown were the original female cast of *Septet*, being revived for the first time since 1964 by the company.

FARBER: We were working in the 8th Street studio—I can't remember what the other piece was.

VAUGHAN: Carolyn, do you? Carolyn gets the prize for longevity, having been in the company from 1952 to 1972.

CAROLYN BROWN: He started *Septet* before we went to Black Mountain [College]. I think we were probably doing the chance piece, the four-part chance piece?

VAUGHAN: Yes, *Suite by Chance* (1953). I think one of the things that's going to surprise people when they see *Septet* is the fact that it is a dance that is done to the music. You didn't learn *Septet* to the music, did you? Because *Suite by Chance* was obviously not learned to music.

FARBER: No, I would have remembered the music part very definitely.

VAUGHAN: So the music was added afterwards, as it is now?

FARBER: Well, Merce must have known what he was doing to what [music]. But we didn't rehearse to the music, because the music was performed live. I don't think we had a tape to it. If John [Cage] and David Tudor came to play—or just David, who could play four hands with two hands—if they weren't there, I don't think we rehearsed it to music.

BROWN: No, not in the beginning. He was experimenting just with movement. But at Black Mountain we rehearsed with David playing both piano parts or with a record of the Satie music whenever David was unable to rehearse with us.

VAUGHAN: Working on material in class, then, seems to be something that happened then and is still done, I think.

GUS SOLOMONS: Probably. I remember learning phrases—dance phrases—in class, but I really have very little recollection of how we learned solo parts and other things. I guess Merce demonstrated them and then right away *extracted* from us individually what he wanted to see. In other words, he would give us an indication of the movement—"This is a hip circle here"—and then he would watch us do it and say how it was wrong and how he wanted it to be done. For me, the process was almost invisible.

VAUGHAN: Yes, it is probably hard to say afterwards how it happened. Gus, of course, was in the company from 1965 to 1968. Before we leave this question of class material, though, is it true that the material was more *squarely* presented in class? Did he then fix it, play around with it?

FARBER: It wasn't so squarely presented in class, as I recall.

SIMON: I agree.

VAUGHAN: I meant *rhythmically* square.

FARBER: That's what *I* mean as well.

VALDA SETTERFIELD: About the solo material: My memory of it particularly with my *Walkaround Time* (1968) solo and also *Changing Steps* (1975), is that Merce didn't show me *anything*. In fact, for my *Walkaround Time* solo, he sat in a chair the whole time and said, "Can you do this? Can you try that? And maybe a little of this, and the other?" It was quite marvelous because I never saw it on anybody else's body—which, no matter how objective you can be, colors your sensibility about it.

VAUGHAN: Valda first danced with the company in 1961 as a sort of apprentice—well, no, you were in the original cast of *Aeon* in 1961—and then was a member from 1965 to 1975. Did Merce work the way she has described with anybody else on the *Changing Steps* solos?

DOUGLAS DUNN: Yes, he hardly showed me anything, either, about the *Changing Steps* solo, and he made me do one thing over and over and over again which I couldn't possibly ever understand. I don't understand to this day what he was asking me to do, but I finally did something that I guess he found okay to leave with me. It's interesting that now someone else does this part. I saw it once and it was . . . I think he had the same take. I guess he got it off the videotape. But I want to tell my own feeling about learning material from Merce. When I joined the company—

VAUGHAN: Doug was in it from 1969 to 1973.

DUNN:—Merce was making two pieces, *Second Hand* and *Tread* (both 1970). I could tell the difference between them because one obviously drove him up the wall, and he was having a good time with the other. The one that drove him up the wall was *Second Hand:* he was trying to make this dance to counts which were coming out of Erik Satie's *Socrate*. Again, he was not playing the music in rehearsal, but he had all the notes in his head, and he was trying to be very precise.

In *Tread,* though, he was being very fast and loose. And in that period, when I was first in the studio to learn these things, Merce was *showing* all material—he wasn't talking any of this material, he was showing it all. I remember standing there, and he was about to show me a phrase. I said to myself, "Now Douglas, watch which foot it is, watch what he does, just watch, watch." And then he would go across the floor, and he would be *here* and then he would be *there,* and I realized that I hadn't seen a single thing that I could take in as mechanics for doing it.

This was some of the most beautiful dancing that I had ever seen and I have no idea if he was making it up on the spot, or whether he had prepared it that morning, or a year ago, or whatever! I have *no* idea. Somehow he got across there in a way that was very exciting and very articulate, but not in a way that I could take in for what I wanted to do. I realized I had a real problem.

VAUGHAN: But this was *before* the dance was performed?

SOLOMONS: Sometimes before and sometimes after, depending on how it looked.

SETTERFIELD: I think, conversely, that sometimes in places where he desired chaos—perhaps we had gotten too comfortable with a passage—he would revert to timing it again, and usually we had slipped and made it slow. By taking it back to its original tempo, the chaos was restored, which made him happy. I think he did exactly what you say—he did both of those things.

BROWN: Perhaps Viola is also talking about two rare occurrences when he *did* use a lot of indeterminacy. One was in *Story* (1963) and the other was in *Field Dances* (1963). We had *so* much freedom in *Story* in terms of timing—or at least we thought we did—that perhaps he thought we were taking advantage of him in certain performances. I remember one situation in which we each had our own phrase to do—it was the "object" phrase—and one of our members stayed out there too long, and he didn't like it at all. He picked her up bodily and walked her off the stage. Because there were certain things that were extremely important to him—especially timing. Timing as part of the total structure of the piece. He has an extraordinary sense of timing and theatrical showmanship.

Another story about *Story*—Steve, can I tell about Cologne? You're *it* for this one. There're lots of stories to tell. In fact, I think Merce is writing a book based on his *Story* journal. We performed the dance all over the world in the 1964 tour. In each place, Robert Rauschenberg made a new set for it, and we rehearsed only the *elements* of the piece, the gamut of possibilities—our steps. And in Cologne—which was somehow a very dark time for Merce on that tour—we needed to be rehearsed, so he asked us to do our slow phrase, as slowly as we could. He went around the room, one by one, and it came time for Steve to do *his* slow phrase. Steve took Merce's instructions very literally, so that a half-hour later, Steve was *still* doing his slow phrase. The rest of us were out in the hallway, saying "Wow, how long is this going to go on?" But Merce had simply taken out his notebook and was looking at his notes, and Steve just kept doing his slow phrase. It was terrific! And Merce was still looking at his notes.

FARBER: Carolyn, that was Tokyo.

BROWN: Tokyo? I remember it in Cologne too.

FARBER: You did it *twice*, Steve?

PAXTON: I did it as slowly as I could. I remember it in Tokyo, too, but that was partly because I had been sick since Warsaw and was still ill in Tokyo. This was four or five months later on the tour—

FARBER: It was the sixth month.

PAXTON:—and at that point, I'm just glad he didn't say "Do it as fast as you can," because probably it still would have taken a half an hour.

DUNN: I was very struck when I was in the company by the intense rigor of the work, the understanding Merce had of the material and the detail—"rigor" is the word I like. At the same time, he was open on various levels at different times and in different situations, to accidents and surprises.

The example that is most personal for me was when we were in a huge gymnasium space somewhere in New England. It was a basketball court, only bigger, and it had bleachers going up both sides—huge! Vast! It must have held two thousand or three thousand people. And there were about twenty people in the audience! We were doing a piece—I don't remember which one—in which I have a run, a big semicircular run, and it was a vast space. We were all struggling to cover this space and make the dance as big as we could to fill the space. I took off to do this run, and right in the middle of it, I slipped and fell, which was totally wrong—it couldn't have *been* more wrong! But somehow, the way I fell, I was able to just roll and get right up and continue running. I was terribly embarrassed. This was the third mistake I had made in a piece in my career at that time, and I was humiliated: this was the worst thing that could have happened to me.

I looked up and Merce was smiling, having seen it, and I realized he dug it. He absolutely loved it. It didn't ruin the piece for him, it didn't cause him to feel that it was out of control. It was beautiful. It fit right in.

SIMON: I don't remember anything ever being changed, or Merce saying "That didn't look good" and then changing it to something else. I just remember that whatever there was, we did it, as close to the speed and counts as he gave it to us. But I don't remember him ever eliminating something because he didn't think it worked.

FARBER: I *do* remember being taught things and attempting to do them, and obviously Merce didn't like how I did them, so he said "Let's drop that."

SIMON: Well, that's because he asked you to do impossible things.

VAUGHAN: What about the repetition part of the rehearsal process? It must really surprise people to see unison passages in a Cunningham work. The unison is so close and everything always comes out together, and yet the dancers don't have any music to hang on to. If you watch Merce rehearse, it always seems to be a very quiet process. Merce sits there, and the stopwatch is ticking away, and the dancers do the piece, and there is very little comment. But somehow out of this comes an extraordinary unity. I think this has always been the case, even if it is true that there is more unison now than there was. Does anyone want to throw some light on this issue?

SETTERFIELD: The rhythms were always so incredibly strong. The audience may not have heard anything, but the rhythms were pounding in our blood.

FARBER: I remember that sometimes rehearsals were very unnerving. Merce would sit and look at his stopwatch, and the only thing he would say when we had finished a dance was "You're a minute too slow." Sometimes we had done other things that could be corrected, and when we were in good shape, we corrected each other in the actual dancing—the shape of what we first time I performed with the Cunningham company—actually, I was doing a part of Viola's. Viola was injured. I had not been in America very long, nor had I worked with Merce very long. I was not informed if I was really going to do the part or if I should learn it, so I hovered around in the back, trying to figure out what to do. Carolyn said to Merce, "Why don't you help her?" He said (she told me later), "I want to see what she'll do with it."

So we went out on the road. We were in a terrible theater where the back curtain didn't come down to the stage floor, and you could see all the crossovers—bare feet going back and forth—and just before I went on, Merce said to me, "This, my dear, is an entrance worthy of Edith Evans. *Take* it." That was actually quite marvelous, because it was something that I absolutely understood, and he plugged into that.

DUNN: Merce often said something about "getting out of the way of the movement." To me there was never any question but that Merce was full of *all* these images and all this feeling about movement. But he did, I feel, restrain himself in general from making comments or suggesting images to the dancers about what he or she was doing, because he wanted most of all to have this directness, this simplicity. Deborah Jowitt used the image of the puppet, not to imply that the dancing is mechanical, but just that the plainness, the simplicity, the directness of movement as such, comes across without the dancer inflecting it greatly.

Merce once said that if the dancer has an idea about the work, something starts to happen, which is not necessarily so good for the dancer. A very interesting aspect of his work is that he gets so much from dancers by leaving them alone in a way that other choreographers do not, so I feel I get glimpses of the dancers themselves inhabiting, in a sense, Merce's world. Because the dancers are *themselves,* to a large extent, they are not becoming characters, and they are not making themselves up if they can help it. In a way you get *more* of the dancers, and that to me is what makes Merce's work go toward life and not completely off into his own fantasy world.

SIMON: I remember that in the very early pieces like *Minutiae* (1954) and *Springweather* (1955) we used to make up endless stories about what we were doing because it was so new for us. Sometimes we would tell him, and he would sort of smile enigmatically, you know. I remember feeling that it was very necessary to have something to hang on to, because it was so new.

BROWN: For the revival of *Septet* (1953), does the program list the sections' names?

VAUGHAN: No, he left those out.

BROWN: It's a very interesting ballet—something akin to Balanchine's *Apollo*, I think. And *Septet* has a very definite story. The section with three couples was called "In the Morgue;" it was about death. Another section is called "In the Music Hall"; another, "In the Tea House." Even when he was thinking about this dance, he had ideas about using candelabras for "In the

Morgue," and ideas of a set for "In the Tea House." But at the point it was beginning to happen, Cage's influence—to have no stories and no narrative—obliterated all that early history of the piece.

Remy Charlip wrote an article for *Dance* magazine [January 1954] about Merce's use of chance processes, and when Remy interviewed Merce he asked him a lot of questions about his earlier solos and the meanings of his solos. And Merce told him a lot of things about meaning, what the dances were about. But . . . it seems that Remy was told not to use that material. Now, *I* think *all* of his dances (and I'm not talking only about through my time there) are about something beyond just "the steps," and, as Douglas says, it's not important either that we knew it or that the audience knows it.

In the article I wrote for the [James] Klosty book [*Merce Cunningham*, 1975], I talked about *Second Hand* (1970), which was the story of Socrates. And it is there. The duet is not actually a duet of male and female; it should be a duet with two males. The story is there, but because the critics—because *everyone* believes what is written about Merce's work, they never looked further to think that, maybe, *Second Hand* was about something *else*—was actually *about* something. It was about Socrates's death, and it was very clear. It was very moving and very touching—the gestures that we all make toward Socrates at the end, dying in the back—it's all there. But everybody believed no, it's not about anything. Some people even said it's something about Graham technique, for God's sake!

Everyone! You shouldn't believe everything that is said to you. You really should not! If you read history books, there's not a whole lot of absolute truth there, either. You have to dig around to find out that there are other things going on in the work besides chance. That's the dogma. I know, but look deeper. There is a *lot* going on there.

FARBER: Douglas, elsewhere you've talked about Merce's "uninflected movement," but I don't quite know what you mean by that. Certainly when one saw Merce dance at the height of his powers, it was not dispassionate, uninflected movement. But there is a difference between putting something on *top* of the movement and letting the movement inform the entire person and, indeed, the entire space. Merce was not someone who was performing only technically exciting feats. Merce was totally *there*, and his character was totally in the movement. No one else danced like that, and in that sense, it *was* inflected. It was passionate; it was very personal.

SOLOMONS: When I was told to "do the movement fully," what that meant to me was to generate an emotion through the movement. But the emotion had nothing to do with some intellectual fantasy; it had to do with the physical feeling the movement gave me. It was never really a problem for me, because I always understood and worked that way myself. I still assume (probably more than I ought to) that people function that way normally.

I always knew inside my secret head that Merce had stories, and that they were very simple and almost silly sometimes. And that was the reason why he wasn't going to tell anybody what they were. Those "stories" helped him make a piece. When the audience saw it, they would put their own interpretation on it and see it in their own way—so why should he get in the way of that privilege which they would have? That seems the way people *should* function. It's a way of admitting the inevitable.

DUNN: I agree with Viola, with her use of the word "inflected." The way I used it was a poor choice of word on my part perhaps. But I agree with the way she describes Merce's dancing. I have a story about something that affected me greatly in this respect.

When Merce made a piece called *Objects* in 1970, there was a section in which about four of us had to sit down on the floor and mime playing jacks, and for the first and perhaps only time in my stint with the company, I was really offended and turned off. I thought, "What the hell is this guy doing? I came here to dance; and he has all this mythology about the steps, and I'm doing it, and that's great. And all of a sudden I'm asked to be a *mime*—something I wasn't comfortable with at all. I don't like that attitude about movement."

Well, we rehearsed this part for weeks and months. Carolyn and I did it—I don't remember who else. Then came the first performance, and I was really resisting. Suddenly, when the moment came to sit down in a circle, Merce *also* sat down. He had never done this in rehearsal, ever, and he had never *shown* us how to play jacks; he just *told* us to play jacks. And in the first performance, he sat down and we took turns. One of us would play and then we would mime (we didn't have any jacks) passing the jacks to the next person. Merce was last, and I had already humiliated myself by doing my turn in resentment. But when it was Merce's turn, he did it so *beautifully* that I was very angry with myself for not realizing that here was another potential.

The point of the story is that Merce has tremendous potential as an actor, a showman, another kind of stage presence. When he dances, he uses it all, but he puts it into the movement; he doesn't use it the way we conventionally think of as acting, or as a mime would. He pushes on it a little bit and it comes out a different way. It becomes ambiguous. "What's going on?" you say—you don't know that he's playing jacks all the time, so to speak. "The expression is in the rhythm," he used to say, which I think was slightly evasive, but it is an interesting comment.

VAUGHAN: He did a wonderful thing in an Event once at the Walker Arts Center in Minneapolis. He mimed making up—putting on stage makeup.

SETTERFIELD: Once in California apparently we had one more performance scheduled than we knew about and Merce did not have enough repertory, so we did an Event. He invited us all to contribute to it and do what we wanted. Everybody was a little shy. We had never worked with him in that way, and he was a little bewildered because we were shy. So he began to organize things, because he was impatient with the fact that everybody was standing there looking timid. But we came to and found things to do. Well, there was a point in it when Merce shaved. Do you remember that? Did he really shave or did he mime?

DUNN: He *really* shaved. He went right down center stage with his makeup stuff and upstaged—or downstaged—us.

SETTERFIELD: It was Merce shaving, but it was also that kind of attention to the brush and the action which was the same thing as when he was dancing. It gave one a real understanding of the fact that everything is important.

DUNN: Once backstage on a little staircase—four or five steps—he did an absolute soft shoe on it. He wasn't afraid to compete with Fred Astaire or Bill "Bojangles" Robinson. That was the only competition.

SETTERFIELD: For me, Merce was awfully good about sharing information. The only thing he needed was for you to ask; he didn't like to tell you things if he thought you weren't ready to understand them. But I asked, and I got the most extraordinary information, even if I had to say to him, "I can't figure out what is going on here, but it isn't feeling comfortable." We would thrash it out between us.

I remember a very straightforward incident when we were doing *Field Dances* (1963), which was originally made for four dancers. Then, when the company got bigger, we all learned those parts so everybody could be in it, including new people. We were doing it in Detroit for schoolchildren in the mornings, and there was a part where a man lay on the floor with his knees up and the woman lay across him, balanced on him, and the kids would call out "Hey, that's sexy stuff." I had a walk that had originally been Viola's, which had a lot of hip rotations in it, and the kids would call out all kinds of sexy things.

So I went to Merce and said, "I think this is really upsetting the balance of the piece. I wonder if I could leave it out." He said "Oh, no. Don't leave it out. If you do, you'll never get it back." And he talked to me about ways to incorporate it into the performance and not upset the balance of things: about maybe not shifting speed, about maybe pursuing the same direction that I was already working in, of paying attention to what else was happening and using somebody else's direction, or working with somebody else at that point. He gave me the most extraordinary understanding of stagecraft and improvisation and composition. He was fantastically generous and incredibly instructive, and I thank him for many, many occasions when he did that.

PAXTON: Getting back to Viola's remark about Merce at the height of his performing power—his extraordinary quality and attention. Last year I saw the company in Santa Fe, where they were suddenly dancing at seven thousand feet, having just come from sea level. They all had the flu and their plane was late—one of those typical disaster times for the company. The first evening of performance left me feeling . . . it's still a great company, but it isn't. . . . The second night was an Event, though, and I was moved to both laughter and tears for the last twenty minutes, because one of the earliest dances that I had learned, bits of *Suite for Five* (1956), was still being done in this Event. My own well-remembered movement, twenty years after leaving the company—still there, amazing! And suddenly being very grateful that I had left the company so I could once again *see* the company, because you *can't* when you're inside. Suddenly feeling that.

Later Merce did a solo, and maybe it's because I imagine that he is in pain when he dances now (I imagine—I have never discussed it with him) and I suppose that it's only years of stage adrenaline that allow him to address the idea of performance at all anymore. But when he started dancing, it was by far the best solo I have ever seen him do in terms of its communicative power. I think it almost might be because of the pain that I presume he is in . . . because he is able to take that in stride and still present this incredible physical manifestation, wherever it comes from. I was completely moved and I felt like Santa Fe had a kind of blessing, as occasionally happens in performance— when the manifestation is so completely clear and present that there is no denying anything, and you're there with it. The empathy with such a performer is such that the entire room is unified and everyone is there, no matter what their circumstances or their own background's pain.

Earlier, the "Caging" influence was mentioned. Once Cage said something about how composition is one thing and performance is another, and seeing a work or being in an audience is yet another. I think that once you step into that kind of appreciation of what's going on, what you as a dancer are trying to convey becomes different somehow, because you don't presume that you are conveying the message that you have *in* you, but rather that each person in the audience is unique; the meaning is always a matter of translation. Just because we are speaking in the same language doesn't mean that we all take in the same meaning. And Santa Fe was an occasion where something beyond reason or meaning in the dance was being conveyed. However, they only got about three bows there; there was no standing ovation at the end, so maybe nobody else was feeling that at all. I don't know, maybe Santa Fe just doesn't *do* that kind of thing—it's so *cool* there.

SETTERFIELD: Sometimes when you see something like that, you are not moved to make a great show of applause. It is a kind of quiet pleasure, for me anyway. So maybe that happened too.

PAXTON: I barely had time enough in those bows to pull myself together so that I wouldn't look a total fool. I would have been sitting there weeping, really. I literally needed the help of the people I was with to get up. We were in the back, so everybody would have seen this guy on the aisle weeping to himself for about ten minutes. I would have stood up and shouted a lot; I actually needed to release the emotion that he had provoked.

VAUGHAN: One often reads that Merce's work has become more or less of something—more balletic, that there is more unison in it, and so on. But it seems to me that, in fact, there is a great consistency. Looking at the company now, what changes do you notice compared to when you were in it?

SOLOMONS: Looking at films of early work, I was impressed with how little the movement has aged, and I wondered why. I haven't thought it through fully, but it is probably because it is so pure in its mechanics that it transcends any date, any time—any fashion—and I think that the purity is consistent. The speed has increased. The attention span—the size of the chunks—has decreased, consistent with our apprehension of the world since television.

PAXTON: The speed has *decreased?*

SOLOMONS: No, speed has *increased,* and the length of phrase has *decreased.* In other words, it comes in shorter shots, because we—the world—now perceive things in shorter chunks, and Merce is part of the world. And that affects what he *does* so well. But it also has to do with the showmanship that Carolyn talks about, because he is the kind of personality that is very aware of the audience and the effect on the audience. He doesn't cater to it, but he considers it in the way he presents what he does. I think that as he has gotten more proficient at understanding that, he has gotten more facile at serving that. I mean, at the beginning, part of his power was to disturb and offend the normal expectations of his audiences, in a way. And that was a way of getting the kind of attention that a performer wants. Over the years, his style has become more magical to people, and he has more power over his audience.

FARBER: I think his work has changed a great deal. As Gus says, the world has changed too, and Merce doesn't work in isolation from it. I left the company in 1965, and in 1970 I did a guest performance with Merce in a work that he had done earlier, *Crises* (1960). That was a five-year gap. I remember watching the rehearsal of the program—the part that I wasn't in, which was everything but one piece—and thinking that the piece from the good old (or bad old?) days must look very strange on that program because it was so different. I felt it would be a very odd program. Since I didn't see it as a program, I don't know if it was. But I very definitely had the impression that Merce had *moved on* to very different kinds of things.

PAXTON: Wasn't that always the case, though? The programs always seemed to me to contain radically different flavors.

FARBER: Really?

PAXTON: From the first programs I saw, there were dances to the music, there were dances to random sounds or prepared piano—whatever John and David [Tudor] had concocted.

SETTERFIELD: You mean *Antic Meet* and *Summerspace* taking place in the same summer, 1958? It was extraordinary.

PAXTON: Yes. . . . The *look* of the thing. Seeing part of *Suite for Five* on the 1986 company with whatever else he had included in this Event (I have no idea

He uses the spine as another *limb*, with equal articulation in all the joints of that spine, and reduces the center from the whole torso to just the pelvis so that the spine becomes free as a limb. But when you look at that movement, at those dances, things are recognizable to you as *arabesque* or *attitude*. But I still think of that as a leg to the back bent, or a leg to the back straight. I may be unique in that perception, but I think it doesn't deserve to be called a balletic style. It's *movement*.

You know, when anybody does something that looks like a curved spine with sharp dynamic, it is called a Graham contraction, whether it is or not. It really should be said that ballet is "Mercean" in style, rather than the opposite.

SETTERFIELD: No, ballet has been going on longer. Give it its due. I think Merce's work is balletic. It is based on the formal structure of ballet, and that was what attracted me to it. When I came here from England, I was thrust into this maelstrom of modern dance which had no clear coherency for me. Then, suddenly, I was placed in a situation with Merce where there was a clear anatomical structure being used, and I understood it; it made sense. We also turned out front, side, and back, as you do in ballet class, doing a warmup which included all the things you did in ballet class, except we called them by an English name and not a French name. The thing that was marvelous was that we worked in parallel to sustain and maintain the alignment more clearly, which held as you turned out. One of the interesting things about Merce is that he is both radical and formal at the same time. I think he needs that. Obviously, he chose a very formal structure with which to begin.

BROWN: I disagree with Gus—that he needed to make pieces to shock. I don't think he ever did that. I don't think he set out to shock, and I don't think he set out to woo an audience. We all need to be loved, but I think his whole choreographic career indicates that he has simply plunged ahead whether anyone liked his work or not. Piece after piece that few people liked. There was a small devoted following, mostly of artists and musicians. But in general, people didn't go, or if they did, they didn't like what they saw. That was the situation for years. It didn't stop him. He never deliberately set out to make a crowd pleaser in his life.

SETTERFIELD: He has a force and a passion that drives him forward, and he was shocked when he shocked people. I think he was shocked once when he shocked *us*.

Carolyn, there was a time after you had left—we had been having class with Merce for years, three times a week at eleven in the morning. The warmup was very formal—structured, slow, thorough, terrific. Suddenly, we got to the center, and all hell broke loose. He began to make phrases that were *miles* long. He would show them once, twice. There were clear landmarks in them. Sometimes one stood still for a couple of beats, or there was a position, or one made a circle—there was something very obvious that one did at some point. He would show them, and he would say "Okay." We hardly knew what had happened, but we would sort of start. One would take something off this person, then another person would remember something, then I'd remember something, and somebody would feed back off me. I thought it was divine! I thought those sessions were the most amazing adventures I'd ever had in my life. I would wake up sometimes in the morning and think "Oh, God, I can't stand an adventure"—but I would get there, and pretty soon I was in *another* one and it was heaven.

However, the company went crazy. People said, "This is irresponsible. This is inappropriate. It could cause injury." Some people said (which I think was the truth), "I don't like being seen not knowing what the steps are." There was a meeting and it was all brought up. Merce got quieter and quieter and quieter as these protests were aired, and finally he said, "I'm trying to find out something for *me*; I've been teaching you for years. I always know what's going to happen. I've been trying to make loose and very dense phrases which I haven't fully worked out. I want to find out what you do with them. I want to find out in the class what is happening."

I said, "I'm having the greatest time I ever had." Everybody else still resisted, resisted, resisted. And he gave those experiments up, because there was not that kind of courage. But I think he was incredibly shocked by the safety-factor needs of the dancers at that time. He had no idea that he was violating something, that he was doing something we wouldn't be comfortable with—no idea at all. And I think that's what happened when he made work: he *made work.* He did not make work for an effect. He did what he had to do.

SIMON: Well, I remember all the way back to *Springweather:* it had a lot of stillness and silence. It was a very long piece for those days. I never saw it, so I can only speak about what it was like from the inside, but it seems to me that the pieces *now* don't have those lengthy, quiet, empty spaces that some of the earlier ones had. Maybe I haven't seen them all, but they seem more dense.

SOLOMONS: The world doesn't have patience for that kind of work anymore—for the stillness.

FARBER: And he has lots more dancers.

DUNN: Well, though, there's *Inlets* (1977); that's a piece that impresses me.

VAUGHAN: *Pictures,* from 1984, has a lot of stillness too.

SIMON: Something that always struck me was that Merce created this wonderful technique for us to learn that *he* never used because he just *danced.* We learned the technique to approximate what he did intuitively. I always found that fascinating, because, when you saw him dance a solo, it was really different from anything that we did as a group. The solo was this creature, just *being.* We, on the other hand, were *dancing.*

ROGER COPELAND: There has always been a distinctive form of concentration visible in the faces of Cunningham's dancers. There are no artificially plastered-on smiles, and there is a certain intense engagement in the business at hand. Is that distinctive concentration in part the result of having danced this horrific and insulting question. (This is my *choreographer*, you know!) And he said that when you commit yourself to something, you do it all the time, not just when you feel like doing it. You have a greater commitment to it than that. That in the times when you don't feel like doing it, you wait—wait until that feeling passes into some other feeling.

SOLOMONS: And while waiting, you keep doing it. That was the important thing, wasn't it?

DUNN: He didn't come out and say it, but that was definitely implied. It was extremely helpful; it was a very generous and helpful statement. While I was there, if you didn't ask you didn't get a lot. If the physical thing was enough, fine; you got that. But the other thing wasn't forthcoming unless you requested it, and it could be quite difficult. There was no way to process verbally—automatically—a lot of the feelings that go on in an intense work situation like that.

VAUGHAN: Did Merce feel that he was developing a technique for purposes other than training his company?

PAXTON: We learned a lot of the dances and a lot of the choreography in class, so the technique—the training method—and the choreography were intimately bound. Whatever he was doing was in a capsule. He could go from balletic work in the center and even movement across the floor into Cunningham choreography—which is supposed to be quite radical—without really having to shift technical gears. I think one of the reasons he did that is that he needed dancers who were there and available through all the rigors of being a dancer . . . which means whether you feel like it or not with the weirdest kind of schedule: lots of classes and rehearsals and performances, perhaps day after day—that kind of physical demand. He needed people who could do that. He knew that, with his training, we could fulfill those demands and dance his dances.

But then the dances, the movement, the development . . . Gus mentioned that the spine was used differently than in ballet, and there were many other differences as well. But I don't feel that all the movement possibilities are there in practice. Carolyn once said that Merce opened more doors for succeeding generations than he cared to walk through, and I think that's possible. But we've seen incredible new influences on movement in this country in the last twenty or thirty years, not only in the developments in modern dance and ballet, but also from the Orient and from Brazil—the Capoieran influence, for example. The movement world right now is broader than it has ever been before in terms of world exchange, so in light of that, Merce's work is quite conservative. (I mean the technical side of it.) Nonetheless, it is fully developed and beautifully made.

BROWN: We have to determine just what vintage of Cunningham technique we're talking about, because the technique itself has changed. It's constantly if subtly changing, depending upon his specific interests at the time. There are basic things that get done generally—the back gets warmed up, the legs get warmed up, and things like that. But, in the very beginning, in the early years when Marianne and Viola and Remy and I were in that tiny little studio on 8th Street, he was definitely exploring his technique—keeping things, tossing them out, finding out what worked and what didn't. The actual continuity of the class changed. There was a time when he did all the back exercises first, and then the legs, to see if *that* worked; then he alternated them. And that hasn't stopped.

When I go to the studio now, I feel that this isn't my home. I really don't identify with what's happening there now in terms of the technique. He is always developing the technique for the choreography. If he couldn't choreograph, or if he stopped having a company . . . since he's said he doesn't like to teach, I wonder if the technique classes would continue to evolve. When he was at the height of his powers, to take his class was so exhilarating it was almost unbearable, because he danced every step of it—he just danced it full out, every step of it. So that what one wanted to do, somehow, was to join that passion. He did not teach us the steps verbally; he never taught us how to do a thing by saying "If you did this and this, then you could do that." You learned by watching him. Some of us had to go elsewhere to find out how to do this awfully difficult stuff.

FARBER: One of his strengths, as a teacher at that time, actually, was that he didn't teach. That was what was beautiful about it! One could get absolutely lost, as Carolyn said, in trying to join him, in this extraordinary thing he was doing. It was just amazing.

BROWN: In the early years, even if we were in Connecticut, we took two classes a day with him, five days a week, and then we rehearsed with him for five or six or seven hours. The Cunningham dancers today go to ballet class; they only get him once or twice or three times a week for class, and of course they rehearse with him. That's different.

When Gus first joined the company (he wasn't an early member), he took the beginning class—I'll never forget it. He was in the company, but he said "I have to know what this is all about." He took the elementary class every day, he took the intermediate class, and he took the company class, because he wanted to know what the technique was about.

Today's company doesn't do that. The whole dance world is different. Martha Graham's people study ballet. Twyla's people—they don't even *have* a modern-dance class. Ballet's been around a lot longer, and I fear ballet's going to swallow it all up—it's going to bland it out.

Oh, I think probably Lincoln Kirstein is right. And since the ballet seems desperate for choreographers and since it's got the institutions and it's got money, and it's got theaters that modern dance doesn't have, it will absorb every new creative imagination it can latch on to.

VAUGHAN: I don't think we can open up that can of worms at this point.

dances named that stress ensemble movement, but also *Changing Steps* (1975), which gives each dancer a solo (and initially these solos were designed precisely to display the individual qualities of the dancers they were made for) as well as featuring them in duets, trios, quartets, and quintets; *Inlets* (1977) which like earlier dances such as *Summerspace, Rune,* and *RainForest* (1968) uses only six dancers; and *Fractions* (1978), which also uses a comparatively small cast (eight) and in its structure reminds one of earlier Cunningham works like *Suite for Five* (1956).

As a choreographer, Cunningham is amazingly and increasingly prolific; in the last year alone he has made three major works, *Inlets, Fractions,* and *Exchange,* the three small *Exercise Pieces* for use in Events or as part of the *et cetera* added in repertory performances to *Changing Steps* (which thus becomes a kind of mini-Event), plus several bits of solo material also for Events, some of which found their way into the new solo *Tango.* And though it is convenient for a critic and historian to group works together and trace lines of development, these recent dances are quite unlike each other in important ways. More and more, it seems almost impossible not to respond to Cunningham's work as drama, and this is as true of most of the ensemble dances as of those with small casts. This doesn't mean, of course, that he has suddenly changed his whole esthetic, abandoned his preoccupation with movement for its own sake, and started to tell stories, but that these pieces have a theatrical intensity that affects one as profoundly as any tragedy.

It is true that their nature as theatre pieces depends to some extent on the total effect of dance combined with music and decor, however independently Cunningham and his collaborators work, and that the dance material when divorced from these other elements, as we see it in Events, may not be easily identifiable as to its source in the repertory. But it is surely true of any choreography that it reaches its full theatrical potential only when combined with one or both of these elements. A lot of the drama in Cunningham's works derives from his own relation to the dancers in his company. The difference in age and agility between himself and the others, who are many years his juniors, is inevitably noticeable in performance. In one way or another, he is removed from them; he appears as a mysterious, controlling presence (as in *Rebus*), as an isolated, even tragic figure (as in *Inlets*), as a leader, or perhaps a tribal elder (as in *Exchange*); in *Squaregame* (1976), he is treated irreverently by the others, getting dragged around and tossed up in the air, but in the duet towards the end he is like some Pygmalion with his Galatea, tenderly guiding and steadying the woman's faltering steps; in *Travelogue* (1977), when he "plays dead," all the others stop in their tracks for a long moment.

Cunningham's relation to the dancers in fact often seems to be the "subject" of a piece. One could take *Sounddance* (1975) as a metaphor for the recent history of the company, or perhaps for the short, intense, often painful span of a dancer's career: the dancers come and go, entering from Mark Lancaster's tent-like structure, starting with Cunningham himself, who is also the last to be sucked back into it again at the end of some twenty minutes of fast and furious activity. That such interpretations of the dance imagery are bound to occur to one shows how nonsensical it is to talk of Cunningham's work as "abstract."

The drama of natural events has been a frequent subtext of his dances, going back at least as far as his first major group piece, *The Seasons*, made for Lincoln Kirstein's Ballet Society in 1947. (As a dancer, Cunningham is one of those, like Duncan, Nijinsky, Pavlova, or Sybil Shearer, who appears to be more a force of nature than simply human.) He returned to this theme in subsequent individual works: *Springweather and People* (1955) and *Summerspace* (1958); *Rune* (1959) was originally to be called *Autumn Rune*, and the tetralogy *manqué* was completed by *Winterbranch* (1964). I have said that the recent *Inlets* resembles *Summerspace*, *Rune*, and *RainForest* in that it has a cast of six; more to the point is its preoccupation with the cycle of time and tide. Its very title suggests the landscape of Puget Sound, and the climate and geography of the Northwest are strongly evoked both by Morris Graves's decor and John Cage's music. (Cunningham originally wanted Graves to design *The Seasons*, thirty years ago, and his first title for that piece was *Northwestern Rite*.) Choreographically, *Inlets* resembles *Summerspace* and *RainForest* in that the dancers move for much of the time as individuals—*RainForest* takes this structure to the extreme of not having any of the dancers return to the stage once they have gone off, except for Cunningham himself; in *Summerspace* and *Inlets* there are frequent entrances and exits for all the dancers.

It is no secret that former members of Cunningham's company and for that matter audience members with long memories find that dances revived from the past, like *Summerspace* and *Rune*, are almost unrecognizable in certain ways. The basic structure may be there, and the steps may be similar in outline to what they used to be, but not in such important matters as rhythm, weight, and phrasing, to say nothing of such intangibles as atmosphere. Such losses are perhaps inevitable with a choreographer like Cunningham, who uses the individual qualities of his dancers so much. Choreographers have notoriously short memories, and notes and even—nowadays—videotapes may not be infallible guides to reconstruction. Anyone who saw Cunningham, Carolyn Brown, Viola Farber, and Remy Charlip in their original roles in *Summerspace* and other dances is apt to find their images so indelible that they superimpose themselves on those of the people now dancing them. But for those who did not, there is no reason why, in *Summerspace*, for instance, Chris Komar, Louise Burns, Karole Armitage, and Robert Kovich should not make an equally strong impression of their own. Certainly the original cast of *Inlets*—Cunningham, Armitage, Ellen Cornfield, Lisa Fox, Komar, and Kovich—is fully capable of giving the work all the weight and atmosphere that Cunningham seems to have wanted for the piece, with its alternations of stillness and activity (he asked that the movement even at its most vigorous should have the quality of stillness).

most of these pieces, he was able to use a larger number of dancers than ever before: his company was enlarged before *Aeon* and *Exchange,* and for *Un Jour ou deux* he was able to use twenty-six dancers from the Paris Opéra Ballet. The scale is large in every sense. *Aeon* had its playful side, especially in some of the inventions in Robert Rauschenberg's designs—for example, Carolyn Brown at one point wore a rope tied around her waist, with various objects hanging from it, a sneaker, a cowbell, a bit of cloth (analogous, of course, to certain elements in his decor for *Travelogue* sixteen years later). *Canfield,* as is well known, was composed according to a process derived from the card game of the same name. Choreographically, though, both *Aeon* and *Canfield* had a kind of majestic sweep and grandeur that made them seem macrocosmic in scale.

Exchange is that kind of work: watching it is like watching history unfold before your eyes. Some of this feeling comes from Cunningham's use of the two generations within his present company: the first section is danced by the more recent recruits, Meg Eginton, Susan Emery, Lise Friedman, Alan Good, Catherine Kerr (returning after a year and a half's absence), Joseph Lennon, and Robert Remley, led by Cunningham himself. Then in the second, these ''junior'' members are replaced by the seniors, Karole Armitage, Louise Burns, Ellen Cornfield, Lisa Fox, Chris Komar, Robert Kovich, and Jim Self. As befits their status as the most senior members, Komar and Kovich at times seem to assume the roles of deputies to Cunningham, the leader himself. Only in the final section do the two groups intermingle, with some switching of partners among the couples.

Exchange, like *Un Jour ou deux,* was designed by Jasper Johns, and shares with it the somber feeling that comes in part from the dark grays of his decors and costumes—relieved in *Exchange* by touches of color in the women's leotards and at the ankles of the men's tights, though even these are overlaid by gray. But in both works, the feeling comes equally from the choreography: there is a kind of sober inevitability as one movement follows another, each moment seems totally realized, so that the overall effect is monumental. The choreography of *Exchange* constantly reorganizes the space not only in terms of area but of volume, displacing whole blocks of air above the stage: it is this which gives the work a positively architectonic sense of weight and solidity. *Exchange* is a major work, worthy to be named in the same breath as Nijinska's *Les Noces,* Graham's *Primitive Mysteries,* Balanchine's *The Four Temperaments,* and Ashton's *Scènes de ballet.*

That Cunningham's latest work should be one of his greatest encourages one to believe that there need be no end in sight to his choreographic career. As a performer, it is clear that he is as much in his element as ever on the stage. His new solo, *Tango,* reminded us, as do his ''Dialogue'' performances with John Cage, that he is one of the great clowns of our time. In recent years, Cunningham has gradually been relinquishing some of his roles to younger dancers. Several years ago Douglas Dunn danced his part in *Winterbranch,* and now Chris Komar dances *Summerspace*, Robert Kovich *Signals,* and the two of them alternate in *Rune.* The breadth and freedom of their aerial movements recall Cunningham's own in former years, even if his magnetism as a performer is inevitably lacking. It may be true that Cunningham himself can do less and less, but he finds more and more ways to do it; one of the exciting things about *Exchange* was that he seemed to have found several new movement possibilities for himself, notably an undulation through the torso, that he will no doubt continue to explore. In any case, the power of his gesture and the authority of his presence are such that he could easily command the stage even if he just stood absolutely still.

Many people have spoken of the irony of the fact that Cunningham, the iconoclast, the *enfant terrible* of yesteryear, out of whose concerts members of the public—not to mention the critics of metropolitan dailies—used angrily to stalk, has now become accepted as part of the dance establishment. As Nancy Dalva remarked in *The Daily Texan,* "Cunningham has not gone establishment, but the establishment has gone Cunningham." It's no exaggeration to say that, in their tours of the United States in the late forties and early fifties, undertaken in conditions of hardship that today's dancers, with their union-set per diems, could not imagine, Cunningham and Cage and, later, the original dance company played as important a role in developing audiences for contemporary dance as Anna Pavlova did for ballet. I sometimes wonder how conscious Cunningham himself is of being a part of the mainstream of dance history—a position many people would have denied him even a few years ago, and possibility still do. That he is a part of it seems as incontrovertible as that he has diverted its course in the second half of the twentieth century.

Changeling, 1957. Photo by Richard Rutledge, courtesy Cunningham Dance Foundation.

Antic Meet, 1958. L to r: Barbara Lloyd, Viola Farber, Shareen Blair, Merce Cunningham, Carolyn Brown. Photo by Fannie Helen Melcer, courtesy Cunningham Dance Foundation.

Summerspace, 1959. Viola Farber and
Carolyn Brown. Photo by Richard
Rutledge, courtesy Cunningham
Dance Foundation.

Summerspace, 1965 production.
Photo © Jack Mitchell.

Nightwandering, 1958; 1965 production. Merce Cunningham and Carolyn Brown. Photo © Peter Moore.

Crises, 1960. Viola Farber and Merce Cunningham. Photo by John Wulp, courtesy Cunningham Dance Foundation.

Crises, 1965 production. L to r: Merce Cunningham, Carolyn Brown, Sandra Neels, Barbara Lloyd. Photo © Peter Moore.

Merce Cunningham and John Cage, 1963. Photo © Jack Mitchell.

The Cunningham Company musician/composers at work.
L to r: John Cage, David Tudor, Gordon Mumma. Photo ©
James Klosty, courtesy Cunningham Dance Foundation.

Merce Cunningham giving a lecture-demonstration at Hunter College, 21 April 1966. Photo ©
Peter Moore.

RainForest, 1968. L to r: Merce Cunningham, Barbara Lloyd,
Albert Reid. Photo © Jack Mitchell.

Arlene Croce

THE MERCISTS (1978)

Spring thaw in New York always brings us the modern dance. Would that it brought us another name for that species of theatrical performance which developed largely outside the spectacular opera-house ballet tradition. Modern dance is, like Romantic ballet, a historical phenomenon. Labels are prejudicial and confining, but we need some other way to refer to dancing that is more than one generation removed from Martha Graham, who is going on eighty-four years old. I have heard "post-modern," and its very weakness and temporariness recommend it. For the recycling age we live in, post-anything sounds right. Actually, in dance there's a fairly explicit tradition that for years has cried out to be called—after its preceptor—mercism. If Ruth St. Denis and Ted Shawn could become a noun (Denishawn), why not Merce Cunningham? We have had mercist companies for quite a while now. Even as Cunningham himself goes on dancing and choreographing, companies headed by his descendants and disciples pop up everywhere. They've been especially ubiquitous in the past few weeks, appearing at Dance Umbrella, at the American Theatre Laboratory (A.T.L.), and at Cunningham's studio in Westbeth. The climax of the series was a two-week stand by the Cunningham company itself at the Roundabout Theatre.

Mercism isn't the only kind of downtown dance activity, and its manifestations are diverse. But generally one identifies it by a commitment to dancing exclusive of music or decor. This commitment to the dancer moving in silence and creating his own space reflects one of Cunningham's paramount concerns—the one that he has held on to longest. Passing concerns of his (happenings, improvisation, non-dance experimentation) recur ghostly in the work of the permanent radical fringe that borders both dance and the spoken theatre. At the moment, we can see one of those periodic inflations of a Cunningham idea taking hold in this sector. Just as the younger generation in the sixties inflated Cunningham's proposition that any movement can become *part of* a dance into "Any movement can be a dance," there are those who are now expanding his insight about the ambiguity of movement into a fascination with ambiguity in all things. Often surface appearances aren't merely allowed to contradict each other, they're directed to. Applied ambiguity blankets many post-modern evenings. One is apt to find more decor than dancing; sound runs to verbal texts. Dance reviews, with their endless speculative remarks about roses that could be noses or whatever the mind supposes, are beginning to mirror the lifeless quandaries posed by these students of the mystique of ambiguity. When faced with one of their impenetrable puzzles, I think of John Cage's advice to Richard Kostelanetz: "Use your experience no matter where you are." It is good advice. Taking the responsibility for the effect of a piece—following what Cage called (in Kostelanetz's book about him) the "non-intentional" aspect—can sometimes be the only way to watch it. And there's always the possibility that what is not intended may be more effective, and even more productive of "meaning," than what is. In Mel Wong's *Harbor*, at A.T.L., the dancing became involved with a display of conceptual art. After about twenty minutes of total inscrutability, I knew I was going to have to get *Harbor* unjammed from an unworkable intention. Wong happens to be a skilled choreographer in the mercist vein, and I found I could enjoy the dancing even though I couldn't tell what it was meant to be about. *Harbor*, though, is far too long to experience just on this level. I couldn't play with pure dance and accidental ambience for the nearly two hours that Wong had chosen to press his intention. As he became more abstruse, with the dancers declaiming numbers or speaking fragmentary sentences or pouring colored water from various plastic containers, I had to become less so—less privately and more professionally interested in what I was seeing. It's not my favorite way of watching, but one can't make mystery out of ready-made *misterioso*. One can't and still hold on to one's respect for the dance craftsman that Wong so truly is.

At mercist lecture-demonstrations, audiences will sometimes ask how much they should know of the creative methods used in a dance in order to appreciate it. The question, not at all a dismissable one, means that they've detected the presence of a process that doesn't disappear into a result. It may also mean that the process looks as if it would be more interesting to watch or to know about than the actual dance it has produced. Process is often deliberately on view in mercist pieces; it's right up there in Viola Farber's works, inseparable from production. My difficulty with Farber is that the process is too obvious: the sectional construction, for instance, that tells me where one day's composing ends and the next day's begins. And one day is as good as another—the process isn't selective. Farber may be the purest mercist around, although I'm told she has no intention of imitating Cunningham's approach to composition. Her work is like Abstract Expressionist painting. You follow it (as you follow all dancing) for the *act* of creation, not for the sake of some disembodied product that creation leaves behind; but you also get the record of what creation involves—you get interruptions and distractions and second thoughts and wipeouts. If Farber were capable of virtuoso brushwork, a long, chuntering piece like *Dinosaur Parts*, seen at Dance Umbrella, might be wonderful. In a new work, *Turf*, she seems to have narrowed and concentrated her means. I watched it with absorption and wondered how much the use of Poulenc's organ concerto alongside the dancing had to do with the relatively flexible and tidy effect. (The David Tudor score used for *Dinosaur Parts* affected me like a dentist's drill.)

Cunningham has initiated more new ideas for theatrical performance than any other choreographer. It's no wonder he has so many followers. Because the material he has brought into being is so richly suggestive, any number can play. When a Cunningham-inspired idea fails, one is still glad it has been tried. Yet ideas by themselves don't make art; they do tend to disappear the moment they're realized. In Cunningham's own best work, as in all works of art, a negotiable idea becomes transparent expression; nothing is left of it but the talent that produced it in the first place. No one who has been influenced by him is working anywhere near Cunningham's level, and one sees—and hears—lots of ideas. Many choreographers, mercist and non-mercist, have tried to get spoken words to work as an accompaniment to dance. The mercist method is to have no direct correspondence between the words and the movement. However, not even Cunningham himself has managed to make them equal partners. Words always dominate; arranged in nonsensical patterns, they still steal the attention away from dance. (The relationship is like that of words to music. Most people identify a song's meaning through its lyric, not through its music. Irving Berlin's "Blue Skies," for example, is a "happy" song, even though its music is a dirge.) Margaret Jenkins, a San Francisco-based choreographer who taught for many years at Cunningham's New York school, collaborates frequently with a poet, Michael Palmer. A voice-over, speaking words in several of the Jenkins pieces that were done recently at Westbeth, forced me to consider meanings that didn't seem to belong to the dances. *About the Space in Between* had a text dealing with Ludwig Wittgenstein, but for me it was really "about" what the title declared it to be about. Jenkins has a keenly sculptural sense of negative space, which she often exploits choreographically both in her own dancing and in that of the group. A void may appear, speaking volumes, only to be retracted, altered, or recharged by a solid shape. Jenkins's dancers are firmly centered (centering to dancers and potters means the same thing), and though not especially wide in turnout, they have a powerful thrust from the inside of the thigh. The strong legs and strong, flexible feet are legacies from Cunningham, emphasized by

Jenkins. Such emphases give these dancers a uniform non-eclectic technique. The foremost mercist company on the West Coast, they appear to be specialists in a very special, insular sense. Not that they're provincial; at least one piece, the epigrammatic *Videosongs*, would have made the reputation of any New York company. But both in the excessively brainy pieces and in the straitened technique there's a little too much hothouse conditioning. More New York appearances would be good for them and us.

A very impressive sound accompaniment to a couple of Cunningham's Events in his Roundabout series was devised by John Cage from his *Mesostics re Merce Cunningham*. The *Mesostics* (a variation on acrostics) are made of words, but they impinge on the ear as pure sound consisting of discrete syllables. Cage published his puzzle poems a few years ago, using within each one many different Letraset typefaces and sizes. He then used the typefaces and sizes as musical notation, letting them dictate pitch, timbre, loudness, and duration. At the Events, the *Mesostic* songs didn't reverse the usual effect of verbal texts on dance, and this was because their performance by the Greek tenor Demetrio Stratos was overwhelming in its virtuosity. Stratos has a voice like no other I've heard; he can switch registers so that they seem to overlap, he can produce drones and ululations with uncanny bell-like overtones, and from a lesser artist than Merce Cunningham he would have stolen the show. I saw the second of two performances with Stratos. Cunningham performed more than he had the week before, when the sound was electronically produced by David Tudor. He was obviously responding to a challenge, and he drew from himself an extraordinary variety of movement, some of it unmistakably and unerringly timed to coincide with Stratos's singing. He is just now in excellent diabolical form, and the occasion brought out his weirdest strokes of wit and drama. He twice held a difficult pose on a bench a very long time while the company danced. He did a slow, foppish solo, full of sly, curlicuing wrists and implied flashes of lace handkerchief. After an appalling minute of complete silence on an empty stage, he entered wearing white coveralls and lay face down, without moving, for another minute. Perhaps his best dance moment was a kind of fractured conga in those same coveralls. Cunningham, now in his late fifties, avoids extremes of movement; he holds to his middle range and makes it seem like a full diapason. All his effects are concentrated, delicate, precise, yet never small. As for the company, the constant addition of new members keeps it looking on the green side, although much individual progress is being made. At the two Events I saw, the choreography was drawn in full or in part from *Torse* (1976), *Winterbranch* (1964), *Changing Steps* (1975), *Canfield* (1969), the wonderful and seldom performed trio called *Cross Currents* (1964), and *Westbeth* (1974), a made-for-TV work. Cunningham's personal repertory consisted of an apparently endless supply of solos that he keeps in his sleeve.

No one who saw Gus Solomons jr, performing with the Cunningham company in the sixties can forget the impact of his tall body and fantastically long legs—as long and thin above the knee as they are below. Solomons could easily have been a male Judith Jamison; instead, he has become a serious choreographer. The company he brought to the Dance Umbrella was the second one of his I've seen; it's young and sunny. Solomons still looks all line, with relatively little muscle—a man who has grown stilts. He did a solo called *Signals* while his music director, Mio Morales, attempted a bit of Demetrio Stratos. *PsychoMotor-Works,* an ongoing company project, had a lot of classical ballet in it, in the form of syllabus positions. Two excerpts were performed; both ended with lively sets of allegro in which Solomons tried for speedy, dexterous footwork—the only one of Cunningham's adherents, as far as I know, to do so. But outside ballet, no one except Cunningham has the secret of allegro. *Bone Jam* was about life experience. It bounced along in episodes broken by blackouts. The dancers, wearing half-masks, appeared in everything from underwear to overcoats, and the movement, which included a good many jokes, ranged from ragdoll limpness to long, clear sweeps and hard, directional changes on a big scale. It was one of what might be called Solomons's junk dances, but there weren't so many bottle caps this time. A good, entertaining piece.

Speaking of life experience, the remarkable thing about the mercists is their esthetic unity. Their backgrounds are widely dissimilar (Mel Wong is of Chinese descent; Gus Solomons jr, is black), and their dancing has been a melting pot. Mercism is really about dancing as experience; it has a built-in dryness and objectivity, and from both dancer and spectator it demands a certain taste for the leaner virtues, for moral disinterestedness. Many people, especially Europeans, find that anti-theatrical. Privileged deprivation may be an exclusively American trait—WASP American, at that. *Théâtre du Silence*, a French company with a modern repertory, opened its New York season (at the Beacon) with a highly unreticent version of Cunningham's greatest lyrical piece, *Summerspace.* The Rauschenberg stippled backcloth was bathed in an orange glow, the sparse piano score, by Morton Feldman, was overamplified, and the dancing was heavy and coarse. It's a company of lusty athletes; one gets the impression that, for the French, avant-garde dance is a form of *le sport* or *le sexe.* Whether they know it or not, the French are temperamentally non-mercist (*non, merci*).

I heard people say that, before they knew better, they took the *Théâtre du Silence* to be a deaf-and-dumb theater. That made me think of Remy Charlip and how much I wish I'd seen his work for the National Theatre of the Deaf and the dances that were derived from it. Charlip was once a member of the Cunningham company, creating roles in *Summerspace* (1958), *Rune* (1959), and *Antic Meet* (1958), among other pieces. He's a noted designer, an illustrator, and author of children's books, as well as a dancer and choreographer, and his gift for visualization and animation stops, apparently, at nothing. There never has been anything like his collaborations, a decade ago, with Al Carmines, the most amazing of which actually wrung a dance oratorio from *The Sayings of Mao Tse-tung*. These days, he is working in theater mostly as a soloist, but in any one of his appearances all his talents manage to be on view. At his Dance Umbrella concert, he began by having his silhouette traced head to toe on brown paper with the arms showing different positions. Then he painted the silhouette blue and flew it as an ensign for the rest of the program. Everything about Charlip suggests consistency, smoothness, and wholeness. His cookie-cutter silhouette, his drawings, and his dances all resemble each other. His art is mime-based, but he is able to draw more abstract inferences from mime than many choreographers can from dance. In *Glow Worm*, he moved about the stage telling stories of his boyhood aloud and using the sign language of the deaf as a counterpoint to both movement and speech. The words, the mime language, and the mime movement supported each other gracefully, but the clear separation between them suggested melancholy dissociation. It's an effect Charlip gets by means of pure mimicry in *Meditation*. As Massenet's insulting, silky music plays on, he slowly contorts his face in a series of agonized or inane expressions divorced from emotional contexts. Charlip works on a very small scale with exquisite balance and discretion. He is someone who might look at home in Japanese ceremonial dress. A lightweight, yes, but also a master.

Merce Cunningham

A COLLABORATIVE PROCESS BETWEEN MUSIC AND DANCE (1982)

What follows concerns a selection of the works that John Cage and I have collaborated on over the past four decades. It is in no sense a complete survey; there are numerous others not included. But these are some of that history that reflect to me a change or enlargement of the underlying principle (with the sole exception of Second Hand *[1970]) that music and dance could be separate entities independent and interdependent, sharing a common time. There is a continuing flexibility in the relation of the two arts. We are involved in a process of work and activity, not in a series of finished objects.*

Whatever tremors it may have provided for the various dancers who have shared these experiences with me, I think they would agree that it is also exhilarating and adventurous. It keeps one on one's toes, and jumps the mind as well as the body.

The first program that Cage and I shared was presented in New York City in 1944. The evening consisted of six solos by myself and three pieces of music by Cage who had also composed the music for the dances.

At the time, he was working in a way he called rhythmic structure, and all of the dances with the exception of *Totem Ancestor* (1942) were choreographed involving this use of time. What was involved was a "macro-microcosmic rhythmic structure" in which the large parts were related to the small parts in divisions of time. This was a way of working between the music and the dance that allowed them to be separate, coming together only at the structural points. For example, in *Root of an Unfocus* (1944), the original phrase was structured 8–10–6 beats. The dance was in three parts, the first section being 8 × 8, the second 10 × 10, the third 6 × 6. The tempo for each section varied as did the time lengths (one and one-half minutes; two and one-half minutes; one minute). This use of a time structure allowed us to work separately, Cage not having to be with the dance except at structural points, and I was free to make the phrases and movements within the phrases vary their speeds and accents without reference to a musical beat, again only using the structural points as identification between us. Each of the five dances made this way had a different time structure and length which came out of my initial working with the movement for the particular dance.

DANCE	TRIPLE-PACED ROOT OF AN UNFOCUS TOSSED AS IT IS UNTROUBLED
MUSIC	THE PERILOUS NIGHT: SIX SOLOS SONGS: SHE IS ASLEEP THE WONDERFUL WIDOW OF 18 SPRINGS AMORES: PRELUDE; TRIO; WALTZ; SOLO
DANCE	THE UNAVAILABLE MEMORY OF TOTEM ANCESTOR SPONTANEOUS EARTH

Studio Theatre, 108 W. 16th Street, April 5th, 1944

I had written *Four Walls* (1944), a dance-play lasting an hour that was to be presented in the Perry-Mansfield Summer Theatre. Cage wrote a piano score for it. I had asked if he could make the score fairly simple, not being certain of the pianist's capabilities in such a situation. We devised a rhythmic structure that included time-lengths for the script and the dancing, and then he composed the work for the white keys only. The rhythmic structure left me free to work with the dancers and actors in such a way as not to pin the words or all the movements to specific notes, although the structural connections were observed. Cage was not present at the summer school, and at one point in the rehearsals, Arch Lauterer, who was co-directing and had designed the set and lighting, pointed out one part he thought too long. "You must cut the music there." I agreed that the section dragged, but did not feel that to cut the music was a solution, and would not have chosen to do so anyway. Searching about for another answer, I changed the dance movements and rephrased the timing of the scene; in other words, used the allotted structural time differently. The next rehearsal Lauterer said, "You see, it is much better with the music shortened."

FOUR WALLS
a dance play

under the joint directorship of
Merce Cunningham and Arch Lauterer

Choreography: Merce Cunningham
Design: Arch Lauterer

Perry-Mansfield Theatre, Steamboat Springs, Colorado,
August 22nd, 1944

In the spring of 1948, Cage and I were touring, giving joint programs of music and dance. One of these was presented on a small stage in the Richmond Women's Club, the "oldest in the country," we were told. The oldest member had been informed ahead of the program about the prepared piano, so that when the sounds were heard she would not be too disturbed. At one point in the program, there was a piece that Cage had arranged for piano and flute. She confided loudly to her companion, "Well, I understand how that other music came out of the piano, but if this one did, then our piano's broken."

Later on that same tour, at a college in Virginia, we were asked to give a lecture-demonstration. We chose not to do the conventional talking and demonstrating, but rather to make a short dance and piece of music in front of the largely student public. Explaining first about the rhythmic structure and what this particular one would be, we proceeded to work separately, he at the side of the stage with a piano, and I in the stage space itself.

As I remember, the structure was 8×8, divided 2–2–1–3. At the completion of any section, any 8, we would try it together, the dance and the music, the public applauding as each point was made. I had explained we did not expect to finish the work, that it was more of an act of process. But we did, to my amazement.

The *Sixteen Dances for Soloist and Company of Three* (1951) was special for me in my work. It was a long piece intended to fill an evening. It was also the first time the use of chance operations entered into the compositional technique.

The choreography was concerned with expressive behavior, in this case the nine permanent emotions of Indian classical esthetics, four light and four dark with tranquillity the ninth and pervading one. The structure for the piece was to have each of the dances involved with a specific emotion followed by an interlude. Although the order was to alternate light and dark, it didn't seem to matter whether Sorrow or Fear came first, so I tossed a coin. And also in the interlude after Fear, number 14, I used charts of separate movements for material for each of the four dancers, and let chance operations decide the continuity.

The work had an overall rhythmic structure to which Cage wrote the score, generally after the dances were finished. He composed it for both piano and small orchestra, distinguished by a number of unusual percussion sounds. Although each dance was a separate entity, we were beginning to use "poetic license" in disregarding connecting points within the dances.

16 DANCES FOR SOLOIST AND COMPANY OF THREE

Solo:	Anger
Trio:	Interlude
Solo:	Humor
Duet:	Interlude
	—
Solo:	Sorrow
Quartet:	Interlude
Solo:	Heroic
Quartet:	Interlude
	—
Solo:	Odious
Duet:	Interlude
Solo:	Wondrous
Trio:	Interlude
	—
Solo:	Fear
Quartet:	Interlude
Duet:	Erotic
Quartet:	Tranquillity

Hunter College Playhouse, January 21, 1951

At the Black Mountain Summer School in 1952, Cage organized a theater event, the first of its kind. David Tudor played the piano, M. C. Richards and Charles Olson read poetry, Robert Rauschenberg's white paintings were on the ceiling. Rauschenberg himself played records, and Cage talked. I danced. The piece was forty-five minutes long, and, as I remember, each of us had two segments of time within the forty-five to perform our activity. The audience was seated in the middle of the playing area, facing each other, the chairs arranged on diagonals, and the spectators unable to see directly everything that was happening. There was a dog which chased me around the space as I danced. Nothing was intended to be other than it was, a complexity of events that the spectators could deal with as each chose.

THEATER PIECE

Speaker: John Cage
Music: David Tudor
Dance: Merce Cunningham
Poetry: Charles Olson
            M. C. Richards
Paintings: Robert Rauschenberg

Black Mountain College, North Carolina, Summer, 1952

Cage had written the pieces *Music for Piano,* the sequence of sounds for which had been found by noting the imperfections in pieces of paper, and applying chance operations to this. I decided to do the same thing to ascertain the space points for a dance called *Suite for Five in Space and Time* (1956). The *Suite* eventually came to comprise seven dances. The spacial plan for each dance was the starting point. Using transparent paper as a grid, a bird's-eye view of the playing space, I marked and numbered the imperfections, a page for each dancer in each of the dances. In the "Duet," the "Trio," and the "Quintet," I superimposed the pages for each dancer to find if there were points where they came together and would allow for partnering or held poses, some form of liaison between them. The time was found by taking lined paper, each line representing five-second intervals. Imperfections were again noted on the paper and the time lengths of phrases obtained from chance numbering of the imperfections in relation to the number of seconds.

This was one of the first dances where meter was completely abandoned, and we, the dancers, had to rely on our own dance timing to guard the length of any phrase, and the timing of a complete dance.

Cage's *Music for Piano,* which was played with the dance, is variable in time. Although the dancers came to know the sequences of sounds, the sounds do not necessarily happen at the same points from performance to performance. And, as sometimes occurred, with the addition of pianists and pianos, the sound was augmented and the original piece had other layers with it.

The total length of a given dance, however, remained identical each time. Through many performances, the duration of the pieces varied little. After a period of, say, three months of not rehearsing, the dancers (assuming they were the same ones, of course) would come within five to ten seconds of a two-minute and forty-five-second dance.

SUITE FOR FIVE IN SPACE AND TIME

the music is from *Music for Piano*

Solo:	At Random
Trio:	Transition
Solo:	Stillness
Duet:	Extended Moment
Solo:	Repetition
Solo:	Excursion
Quintet:	Meetings
Solo:	For the Air

The events and sounds of this ballet revolve
around a quiet center, which, though silent and
unmoving, is the source from which they happen.

Piano: David Tudor
(First Performance)

The University of Notre Dame Concert and Lecture Series, May 18, 1956

My company and I were in residence at Connecticut College in 1958, and
there was to be a festival of programs the last week. We would appear on two
of them. So I made two dances, *Summerspace* with a commissioned score from
Morton Feldman, and the second, *Antic Meet*, using Cage's *Concert for Piano
and Orchestra*. This was one of the first times I gave him only the length of the
total dance (twenty-six minutes), but no time points in between. His score is
indeterminate in length, and also in the proportions within the piece, so even
though the dance was set, we could not count on the sounds as cues, as they
never fell in the same place twice. The dancers' unsupported timespan was
expanding.

ANTIC MEET

Merce Cunningham, Choreography
David Tudor, Pianist
John Cage, Conductor
(First Performance)

Connecticut College, New London, Connecticut, August 14, 1958

The *Events* were originally intended as a means of giving performances in
unorthodox surroundings. Since then they have sometimes been given in

conventional theaters. The first *Event* was presented in the *Museum des 20 Jahrhunderts* in Vienna during a world tour. The music was Cage's *Atlas Eclipticalis* and was played by six musicians who were seated apart from one another in the corners of the large hall in which the *Event* took place. Since the performing area was unconventional, just an open space in the museum, it did not seem to us that a conventional presentation of three or four dances was appropriate, and so we chose to present a single length of time, an hour and a half, in which the music and the dance could be heard and seen. I put together a series of sections out of the repertory. At times during the program there were several dances going on at once. There was no separation between the dances; we went directly from one to another. The audience was seated mainly in front of us, but also extended onto the two sides. The musicians played continuously for an hour and a half. Since we, the dancers, had no awareness of what the continuity of sound would be, we were free to involve ourselves in what we were doing.

We continue to present *Events* in orthodox and unorthodox situations, usually with four musicians. In recent years they have been Takehisa Kosugi and Martin Kalve as well as Cage and David Tudor. Each is a composer, and each makes a sound ambience separate from the others, using the *Event* time as he chooses. The dance material now consists not only of pieces from the repertory, done in whole or part, but also dances and actions made specifically for the *Events*.

MUSEUM EVENT   VIENNA 1964

Mittwoch 24. Juni 1964   19:30 Uhr
Gastspiel
Merce Cunningham & Dance Company, New York

Museum Event Nr. 1
(Erstauffuhrung)

Tänzer
Merce Cunningham

Carolyn Brown   Viola Farber
Shareen Blair   Deborah Hay   Barbara Lloyd   Sandra Neels
William Davis   Steve Paxton   Albert Reid

Schlagzeug:
John Cage
Friedrich Cerha
Peter Greenham
Judith Justice
Petr Kotik
David Tudor

Musik: John Cage (*Atlas Eclipticalis*, 1961/62)
Dekor, Kostüme, Beleuchtung: Robert Rauschenberg, Alex Hay

The French-American Festival had commissioned Cage to prepare a score and me to make choreography for it. For this work, *Variations V* (1965), Cage decided to find out if there might not be ways that the sound could be affected by movement, and he and David Tudor proceeded to discover that there were. Several, in fact, only two of which finally worked out for use in the piece, the rest being impractical due to cost, or requiring machines not usable in the theater, or simply too clumsy. The two ways that were used were not differentiated with respect to the dance, but were different for the musicians, the technicians, and the stage set-up. The first was a series of poles, twelve in all, like antennae, placed all over the stage—each to have a sound radius, sphere-shaped, of four feet. When a dancer came into this radius, sound could be triggered. Each of the twelve antennae had different sound possibilities. The metal rods were five feet high and roughly one inch in diameter. I had not known the exact dimensions of the poles nor their placement previous to the stage rehearsal the day before the performance, as the technique necessary to ready them had been in a constant state of experimentation, but I did know they would be upright and the number would be twelve. So I had prepared the choreography and the dancers—there were seven of us—for the possibility of instant changes of mind. But I did wonder about our feet stepping on the wires which would be running from the base of the poles across the floor and up to the electronic systems which controlled all this. Fortunately, it was a surmountable impediment.

The second sound source was a series of photoelectric cells which were to be positioned on the floor along the sides of the stage. The stage lights would be focused in such a way as to hit them, and when a dancer passed between the cell and the light, more sound possibilities were triggered. This did not work out precisely, as the stage lights were too distant to strike the sides of the stage strongly enough. After all, they were focused on us and we were prone to be in the middle of the area. So at the last minute the cells were put at the base of the twelve poles throughout the area and this was a viable solution. The general principle as far as I was concerned was like the doors automatically opening when you enter a supermarket. The dancers triggered some of the sound possibilities, but the kind of sound, how long it might last, the possible repetition or delaying of it, was controlled by the musicians and technicians who were at the numerous machines on a platform behind and above the dance space. They utilized tape machines, oscillators, and short-wave radios.

Film and television images were also used in this work. Stan VanDerBeek and Nam June Paik both showed visual elements on screens behind and to the side of the performing area. There were also various props: a plant, a pillow, a pad, a table, and two chairs, to which contact microphones were attached and which, when moved or touched by the dancers, added to the sound possibilities. At the end of the piece I rode a bicycle, the wheels wired for sound, through the space, around the poles and the photoelectric cells, and then exited.

New York Philharmonic

French-American Festival, July 23, 1965 at 8:30

John Cage: *Variations V*
(World Premiere)
Merce Cunningham, Carolyn Brown, Barbara Lloyd, Sandra Neels,
Albert Reid, Peter Saul, Gus Solomons jr
    Electronic Devices: Robert A. Moog
    Film: Stan VanDerBeek
    Distortion of Television Images: Nam June Paik
    Technical Consultant: Billy Klüver
    Musicians: John Cage, Malcolm Goldstein, Frederick Lieberman,
               James Tenney, David Tudor
    Lighting: Beverly Emmons

One of the earliest of my solos, called *Idyllic Song* (1944), was made to the first movement of the *Socrate* of Erik Satie. Cage had arranged the music for two pianos. Over the years, he had suggested I choreograph the other two movements, as he had planned to arrange them for piano also.

On one of our tours in the late sixties in the Middle West, David Tudor and Gordon Mumma, the musicians with us, explained to me that it was difficult for them to make different electronic set-ups for each of three separate dances for the performances and what could be done about it? Cage suggested I choreograph the *Socrate*. He had completed the two-piano arrangement. I worked on the dance, remembering the early solo for the first part, making a duet for Carolyn Brown and myself for the second, and a full company dance for the final movement. A month before the scheduled first performance, Cage telephoned from Davis, California (where he was in residence at the University of California) to say that the Satie publisher had refused permission for his two-piano arrangement, but not to worry as he was writing a new piece for one piano, keeping the structure and phraseology of Satie's music but otherwise using chance operations to change the continuity so there would be no copyright problem. When he told me this, I replied, "But you will have to rehearse with us and play the music so we can learn the new continuity." "Don't worry, I will," he answered, "I'm calling my version *Cheap Imitation*." "Well, if you're dong that, I'll call mine *Second Hand*." It was the last time I made a work following the phraseology of a musical score.

Second Hand	John Cage
	(Cheap Imitation)

(First Performance)

Part I	
Merce Cunningham	
Part II	
Merce Cunningham	Carolyn Brown
Part III	
Merce Cunningham	Carolyn Brown
Sandra Neels	Valda Setterfield
Meg Harper	Susana Hayman-Chaffey
Jeff Slayton	Chase Robinson
Mel Wong	Douglas Dunn

Decor: Jasper Johns
Piano: John Cage

Brooklyn Academy of Music, January 8, 1970, 8:30 P.M.

In the fall of 1973, I spent nine weeks in Paris working with dancers from the Opéra Ballet. The *Festival d'Automne* and the Paris International Dance Festival had jointly commissioned this work to be choreographed utilizing dancers from the Opéra on the Opéra stage. I asked Cage if he would compose the music, and Jasper Johns if he would design the decor. They agreed. It was to be an evening-length work without intermission and would involve the full Opéra facilities. The work was to be called *Un Jour ou deux*.

Cage had originally wanted to use the works of Satie in various juxtapositions, to make a circus of Satie's music, but Salabert, the publisher, refused permission. So he composed the work *Etcetera*, for orchestra, which involved twenty musicians and three conductors. Cage arrived in Paris a month before the first performance, and proceeded to have consultations with Marius Constant, the principal conductor, and the other two, Catherine Comet and Boris de Vinogradow. When the first musical rehearsal came, there was a problem. From what I understood, the musicians, upon learning that they were to make choices about which sounds they played, as indicated in Cage's score, asked for more money, pointing out also that it was chamber music. Rolf Liebermann, the then Director of the Opéra, spent a good part of the day with them, eventually solving the difficulty by giving them two marks (double pay) for each rehearsal and performance. Cage was worried about setting a precedent. Constant said, "Don't. It's the Opéra. It would have happened anyway."

Each day, I was in the top of the building working in the ballet studio with the dancers, many of whom were worried about dancing without musical support, and what would happen when the two came together? This fear increased as the piece grew longer, one or two of the soloists becoming quite upset at times. I thought it had to do mainly with an idea about their image, and assured them they were strong enough as dancers not to be thrown off by it.

At the first rehearsal of the music in the theater without the dancers, a sound like rain on a number of roofs came out of the pit. The large handful of spectators rushed forward to see what was producing it. Each musician had, as a supplement to his instrument, a French cardboard carton which he used as a drum at various moments during the piece.

Several days later, at the first full rehearsal of the work with the dancers on the stage and the musicians in the pit, I had to repeatedly calm several dancers as to their dancing with the music. Finally the rehearsal began. I was nervous enough trying to keep track of the dance and the timings within it and what was working and what wasn't, so any difficulties they might be having with the music were not immediately apparent to me. Afterward, upon my questioning, they said, "The music? No, we didn't have any trouble."

UN JOUR OU DEUX

Choreography by Merce Cunningham
Music by John Cage: *Etcetera*
Decor and Costumes by Jasper Johns
Assistant: Mark Lancaster
Conductors: Catherine Comet,
Marius Constant, Boris de Vinogradow

Théâtre National de l'Opéra, Mardi 6 Novembre 1973 à 20H30

Our *Event for Television,* presented on the National Educational Television's "Dance in America" series, was a collaboration among the dance company, John Cage, and David Tudor. This was an hour program which in this instance became fifty-eight minutes and forty-five seconds. Charles Atlas, with whom my video and film work has been done, and I spent four weeks working out the dances and excerpts of dances we planned to present. The excerpts that were from the repertory were remade and angled for the camera; in some cases they were shortened, as I feel one receives information quicker and more directly on television than on the stage.

Cage and Tudor decided to share the hour, Cage having the first section for which he played *Branches,* music for plant materials. He was interested in sounds from nature and had found that the spines of cacti, when touched and amplified, produced resonant sounds. At the point in the program, when the dance *RainForest* (1968) appeared, Tudor's music for it began, and this continued through the balance of the hour. Both musics were introduced into the program after the taping and editing had been completed—that is, several weeks after the actual shooting of the dances.

Working with dance in video requires a constant adjustment in terms of space, often on a small scale. A six-inch shift can seem large on the camera.

This also can cause a displacement in the timing requiring a change in rhythm, or the amplifying of a dance phrase, sometimes necessitating a cut or speed-up of the movement. In the conventional music-dance relationship, this could require a constant recomposing or rearranging of the sound. But since I work separately from the music and not on a note-by-note relationship, I was free to adjust the dance phrases and movements through the camera in a visual sense.

EVENT FOR TELEVISION

Minutiae
Solo
Westbeth
Septet
Antic Meet
Scramble
RainForest
Sounddance
Video Triangle
Music: John Cage (Branches)
David Tudor (RainForest)
Taped at Nashville, Tennessee, 8–11 November 1976
First public showing, WNET/"Dance in America," 5 January 1977

The most recent collaboration that Cage and I have been involved with was the International Dance Course for Professional Choreographers and Composers held in August 1981 at the University of Surrey in Guildford, England.

The workshop was a two-week period that involved eight choreographers selected by audition from professional companies (ballet and modern) on the Continent and in the United Kingdom, and eight practicing composers, with a nucleus of twenty-seven dancers and five musicians for the various choreographers and composers to use as working personnel in the projects.

With one exception, Cage and I decided to conduct the workshop by means of chance operations. The exception was the time length of each project. The decision here was to make the original project four minutes in length and to increase the daily project by a minute; thus, the final project would be fifteen minutes long.

Other than this, the rest of the decisions concerning the daily work were decided by chance operations: the number of dancers or musicians any choreographer or composer would work with each day, the actual dancers and musicians involved in a given piece, and the composer-choreographer relationship.

Each day after the morning class and lunch, I would suggest a project to the choreographers and dancers from ideas I had employed in dances in the past. These ranged from simple time and space problems to complexities involving multiple spaces and superimposition of movements and phrases.

Then each choreographer would be informed as to the number and names of the dancers he or she would be working with that day. The dances ranged from solos to octets. Following this, the choreographers had the balance of the afternoon, roughly three to four hours, to work with their dancers in the separate studios the university provided.

With the composers and musicians, Cage talked each morning about the ideas in his music. He gave a survey of it from the earliest pieces to the latest work, pointing out the musical ideas he had been working with in each instance and the philosophical concerns with which he had been involved. He did not present a particular project to the composers, preferring to leave them free to make their own choices.

Neither the choreographers nor the composers knew during the afternoon working period which music would be played with which dance.

Each evening for the twelve days of the workshop there was a program of the dances and the music that had been made during the day. And it was then, again using chance operations, that the decisions were made as to the choice of music to be played with any given dance. At times, there would be two choreographers' works being presented to a single composer's music. At other times, two separate pieces would be played along with one of the dances.

One came to the evening's program with a certain amount of anticipation and, although not all fare was gourmet, there were an astonishing number of times when the music and the dance seemed to have been made for each other.

The original plan of having a minute added to the length of the works each day was relinquished after the first week. A number of the choreographers felt it was difficult to deal with the increased length each day due to the short working period and their unfamiliarity with the dancers. They made their own decisions about the length, although several of them elected to continue the one-minute addition. And choreographers who, during the first week, had worried about doing a longer work each day, found a ten- or twelve- or fifteen-minute length not intolerable, but provocative and feasible.

The sharing of dancers, musicians, and ideas; the non-impinging atmosphere that resulted (as well as the extraordinary amount of music and dance that was made, rehearsed, and presented each day) was exhilarating, giving a feeling not of things finished, indexed, and catalogued, but of work that was being done, and could continue to be done and shared.

INTERNATIONAL DANCE COURSE FOR PROFESSIONAL

CHOREOGRAPHERS AND COMPOSERS

University of Surrey, Guildford, England

Sunday 16th August–Saturday 29th August 1981

David Vaughan

LOCALE:
THE COLLABORATION
OF MERCE CUNNINGHAM
AND CHARLES ATLAS (1981)

Merce Cunningham often speaks of the profound impression that the films of Fred Astaire made on him when he was growing up in Centralia, a small town in the state of Washington. Astaire was concerned with the dance for its own sake, and was always trying out new ideas, new rhythms, new steps—it is said that he used to screen his old movies frequently to make sure he would not repeat himself. Cunningham, throughout his forty years as a choreographer, has also pursued a restless search for new ways to move.

In recent years Cunningham has emulated Astaire in another way—when he went to Hollywood, Astaire decided that he had better learn the craft and technique of filmmaking if he wanted to keep control of the way his dances were shown on screen. Cunningham made a similar decision with respect to video when it became clear to him that this was a medium that would allow his work to be seen by a wider public. As early as 1961 he had choreographed a short work for Canadian television, and there were telecasts during the Cunningham Dance Company's 1964 world tour (including one of a live performance in Helsinki, from which *Story* [1963] is now distributed as a film by the Cunningham Dance Foundation). In 1968 Cunningham choreographed *Assemblage*, filmed on location in Ghirardelli Square, San Francisco, under the direction of Richard Moore, for KQED-TV. But in these cases Cunningham raphy of *Locale*—"communication as direct and transparent as any we have had on film since the hand of Picasso drawing in *Le Mystère Picasso*."

Perhaps to simplify things for the spectator by not forcing him to register too many different kinds of movement information at once, Cunningham choreographed his first section mostly in terms of stop-motion poses. The second section begins with a sequence of short passages separated by cuts, during which the movement becomes more fluid. (In the first section whatever cuts are necessary are made as unobtrusively as possible, usually at moments when the camera passes a blank wall.) The timing of the editing here is often virtuosic, as when Joseph Lennon leaps off some steps, crashes to the floor, and immediately Lise Friedman is lifted by Alan Good—the surprise of this sequence of movements works perfectly on camera in a way that it never can, quite, on stage. In a later section, the camera moves again, at one point executing a complete 360-degree revolution around the studio space, finding dancers in corners or catching their reflections in the mirror, that is as techni- cally dazzling as the opening shot of Max Ophüls's *Madame de . . .*

The making of *Locale* was recorded in a brief documentary by Atlas called *Roamin' I* (which can be read as Roman One or Roamin' Eye), consisting of some material specially shot during the filming as well as outtakes from *Locale* itself. This is a hilarious and instructive glimpse behind the scenes, or behind the camera, showing the dancers scuttling around to make their re-entrance on another side, climbing over cables, jumping out of the way of the dolly or crane. An elaborate system of pulleys was devised to pull the cables out of shot as the camera pursued its restless path, and one sees this in operation, with the accompaniment of shouted cues to the technicians in charge. (The sound- track of *Locale*, which consists of electronic music and some ambient sound recorded during the filming, was added later.)

The latest Cunningham-Atlas collaboration, *Channels/Inserts* (1981), has already been seen on stage, during the Cunningham company's recent City Center season. The film is, at this writing, still being edited. This time the collaborators used the entire premises of the Westbeth Studio, not just the main studio itself. The stage version is certainly among Cunningham's most impressive recent works; word is that the film version will look very different, which is certainly true of *Fractions* and *Locale*, but one may be sure that it will yield plenty of surprises.

Cunningham's work as a choreographer has been based on an innovative approach to the nature of time and space in the theatre. For instance, he rejected the notion, proposed in Doris Humphrey's book *The Art of Making Dances*, that certain areas of the stage are "weaker" or "stronger" than others, and the time element of his dances is not governed by conventional notions of "build-up" and climax. It is not surprising, therefore, that he has shown an instinctive grasp of the nature of these elements as they are perceived in video, realizing, for instance, that time can be treated elliptically because the spectator absorbs information much faster than in the theatre, and that space appears to widen out from the small aperture of the screen, giving an illusion of greater depth than in fact exists. Cunningham's video pieces are composed with such characteristics in mind. (Other choreographers have "reconceived" their works for television, but Martha Graham, for instance, in reworking her *Clytemnestra*, retained sequences whose repetitiousness seems excessive in terms of television "time," while George Balanchine has usually preserved the symmetrical spatial configurations inherent in the balletic hierarchy.) Cunningham is the first to agree that dance on the screen can never have the immediacy of a live performance, but his video and film dances prove that work in those media can have a vitality of its own—just as Astaire's did.

Merce Cunningham

DIARY OF A CUNNINGHAM DANCE (1981)

During the six-week work period of the film/dance that Charles Atlas and I have made, I kept a diary of the work in progress, *Channels/Inserts*.

It was understood from the beginning that this work would also be performed on stage during our two-week season at City Center, and that the stage adaptation would be made after the camera version had been completed. For the stage you have to choreograph entrances and exits, whereas with film you need only shift the camera to eliminate a dancer.

The piece, the fifth Mr. Atlas and I have filmed in my studio at Westbeth, was to be twenty-eight minutes long after editing. He and I planned all the cuts in advance, and all filming was done with those in mind. Three cameras were available: a still camera—that is, one in a fixed position; a "dolly," a camera mounted on a small wheeled platform to be moved during filming; and the third, a Steadicam. This last was a camera suspended in front of Charles Atlas, who wore a brace to support it and was able to move about freely while using it.

The work is comprised of sixteen sections varying in length from ten seconds to three minutes. Each section has a different number of dancers, although six seem to predominate.

Herewith my jottings:

Dec. 23—First day of rehearsal with the dancers. Labyrinths of notes and drawings I've made working by myself during the past months to turn into steps and placements. After three hours with five dancers, we had a little more than a minute of the complete work—two couples and a girl dancing in an eight-foot diameter of space (disco in an elevator).

I will work with the dancers during the week, Tuesday through Friday, using a small viewfinder as a helper, and the filming will be done on the weekends when the dance studios are freer from their ordinary allotment of classes. The various sequences are to be shot mainly in our large dance studio, with several being made in the small studio and in the corridor running between them.

Dec. 27—Camera work is basically uncooperative with dancing—limbs getting out of the camera frame. The dance is to be shot in both film and video, the film for eventual broadcast possibilities and the video for instant playback, essential for seeing what it is you've done.

Dec. 28—I tried out some fragments for the long two-minute corridor sequence. It has all the dancers in couples appearing in and out of doorways. Where do they go when the camera gives them only walls and inches?

Jan. 3—First time with all the dancers and the whole crew. There are twenty-two of them with Charlie Atlas, the two cameramen and assistants. And fifteen of us. Big production. Rehearsing for filming. At first glance through the cameras, nothing works. All the angles are wrong: try again. Then all the cameras and monitors go blank; so while remedial practices are applied to the instruments by the crew, I work on a section for the men—a still camera sequence with the dancers leaping into and out of camera range.

Jan. 4—Long technical day. Constant attention is what it's about. No arm let go, no pose thrown away. Charlie's continued concern for each single shot is admirable if exhausting. But dance on camera seems to require this or it stumbles. Also we are planning the cuts from one camera to another, and this requires a stop or a clarification of the dance action to make the cut possible. A cut in film takes the place of eye-shift in theater.

Jan. 5—Sat with Charlie looking at the video playbacks of Sections 1 through 4, watching for technical errors and ways to enliven the angles. Dancing on film doesn't seem to have presence.

Jan. 6—I started on another section, this one with three couples again. Looking through the camera at what I'd made previously, muttering to myself, "That phrase has to be re-angled; now Karole's too far out; if Cathy and Robert move over and the rhythm is quickened there, the three couples are O.K.; why's this look so flat?; oh, that works!; but wait a moment! stop! stop!" Go back and begin again, almost frame by frame, and after a half-hour of that, where's the dance life?

Jan. 9—After years of watching dancers in the flesh, it is still difficult for me to turn my back while they are dancing and see them only in the monitor.

Jan. 10—The first film shooting day. The dolly is moved onto the dance floor, the camera positioned, the decks and monitors stretched out on the edge of the space. One of the cameramen stoops over the dolly, hands on the handle ready to push it along the floor. This bent-over position is his for the next three weeks. He manages it with humor.

Jan. 11—The studio is completely changed. The company room's a costume and make-up headquarters; the women's dressing room has become a small café complete with coffee urn and bench covered with croissants, fruit, and cheese, and various members of the crew and company munching. Charlie's room is full of film equipment, and the main studio has become this black walled and floored vault. No light from outside allowed to enter.

After two days of shooting, we have about seven minutes filmed.

Jan. 15—I asked the dancers to go through what we had of the piece, some twenty minutes, to give them the chance to do something fully and give myself the opportunity to see it. Great deal of activity.

Jan. 16—The sound engineer tapes "room sound," the ambient noise, with each take. This will be added during the editing, as will the music being composed by David Tudor. Since my choreography is not set to music and not governed by musical phraseology, I am free to change it as need be in terms of camera angles and cuts.

Jan. 19—We had about twenty minutes' rehearsal on the thirty-second sequence in Section 3 where the Steadicam is used. Charlie, rushing about in the midst of the gyrating dancers, with that brace on and the camera suspended in front of him, looks like some large leaning animal trying to avoid collision with a bunch of humans each going in a different direction.

Jan. 22—Grand entertainment in a way, this dance/film experience. Shocks the sense of time, and makes one aware of minute differences—like lengths of arms. How'd they get so long? Dancers have an automatic way of putting arms out to balance and counterbalance what the rest of the body may be doing. But often on the camera they have to do the opposite to keep them in view—moving toward the edge of the space and dropping an arm instead of raising it to the side.

Jan. 23—The studio has a black cavernous look now with the curtain drawn totally around, the stage framed in black flats, the floor covered with black marly. It takes an hour after the morning class to ready all the curtains, flats, lights, and cameras before the dancers appear. Then there's about two-and-a-half hours to try as much as we can, with the dancers and the equipment, before it all must be removed, the window shades lifted, the piano pulled out of the corner, the floor cleared, and casts exchanged—crew and company leaving as students troop in with dance bags and aspirations. The teacher appears, the pianist begins, and there is again the formality of a dance class.

Jan. 24—"What's that on the floor? Is that oil?"
"The dolly's leaking."
"Dancers, sit down and relax!"

Jan. 25—Getting dance on camera is a process that demands constant attention in multiple directions, during the brief period of a shot—say ten seconds to three minutes—and immediately afterward looking at the video playback to note omissions (loss of a hand, a lift cut, an angle that covers one of the couples), and the undesired additions (top of the curtain, an inadvertent foot from the sidelines, a flare in the lights). The dancers have maintained a remarkable calm under the weeks' strain. After the fifth take of a sequence which has gone well for them, ill for the camera, they do it again with good spirits.

Jan. 27—I saw a sampling of the footage from the Steadicam episode in the corridor. Like a ride on a horizontal roller coaster. Some of the shots in the tape look O.K., giving us some confidence in the eventual product.

Jan. 29—One of the odd things about working in this medium is the time differential. The performers have finished the show, but the public can't see it until several months elapse. Charlie's editing intervenes.

Feb. 1—Final shooting hours. We started at noon and ended at 8 P.M. The last shot was of a duet in the small studio, with the Empire State Building out the window as a backdrop. The dancers exit, and Charlie sets up a special camera which uses a time-elapse mechanism, and which, operating through the night, catches the Empire State lights going off at midnight and the change as dawn arrives. He plans to run it under the credits.

"All right, everybody, one more time."

"What take's this?"

"Seven."

"O.K., ready; roll tape, Jenny."

"Dancers in position; silence; roll sound."

"Speed."

"Slate it, Bob."

"Roll camera."

"A one insert 3, take 7, sound 195."

"Dancers, ready."

"Go!"

Don Daniels

CUNNINGHAM, IN TIME (1985)

To see the American Ballet Theatre production of Merce Cunningham's 1980 *Duets* is to see Cunningham acquired by the ballet boutique. At ABT, Cunningham's repertory staple becomes a prestige item. At best, it's a remedial exercise for deprived ABT dancers. (Where else in the rep—so goes the apology—can ABT's budding soloists encounter equivalent challenges?) The Met audience reacts with the mildness it brings to all the seasonal imports on display. Although *Summerspace* (1958) may not have settled in at New York City Ballet back in the sixties, today *Duets* does so with ease across the plaza. And, at ABT, it's not merely a matter of stylistic subtleties lost in the transfer. Rather like the recent ABT production of Balanchine's *Symphonie Concertante*, everything is there but the dancing.

Take, for example, the perception of the metrical weight of Cunningham's dance style. By "weight" I am not referring to a physical weight used by performers in the production of Cunningham dance on stage. (Cunningham's dancers are asked to use their *ballon* with more variety, and more regularity, than the ballet-trained ABT dancers.) I mean something like the viewer's awareness that the dance has an insistent metrical order. Dance metrics govern Cunningham's work, aid in its production, sometimes even become the preponderant expressive element out of several (attack, dynamics, *plastique*, etc.). I know trained dancers (with no background in Cunningham classroom training) who say that they can "count" a Cunningham dance while watching it being performed. I'm not sure that this is literally true, but I think I know what they mean. With no immediate or detailed competition from conventional musical accompaniment, Cunningham rhythms are exposed and "held" in a way that dance audiences may sometimes find assertive. The very charm of this exposure—its blatancy and frankness—allows the audience a sensitivity to dance rhythm that can startle. It seems so at times to me—for example, in Cunningham's large-scale ensemble works like *Torse* (1976) and *Rebus* (1975). When Cunningham himself or his best soloists perform his best material, they add many rhythmic values, lighten the texture, complicate it. On the other hand, when the group performs in concert, basic principles are nakedly revealed, and the Cunningham metric can seem flatly rhetorical.

In this respect the Cunningham approach to dance rhythm may derive from John Cage. Cunningham and Cage met in 1938, one year before Cage's composition *First Construction (in Metal)*, a score organized according to durational proportions—the relationship of temporal lengths in musical materials. In a lecture delivered in 1948, Cage summed up this durational approach to structure: "There can be no right making of music that does not structure itself from the very roots of sound and silence—lengths of time."[1] As late as the *String Quartet in Four Parts* (1950), Cage continued to use a "rhythmic structure": "Sounds, including noises, it seemed to me, had four characteristics (pitch, loudness, timbre, and duration), while silence had only one (duration). I therefore devised a rhythmic structure based on the duration, not of notes, but of spaces of time. The whole has as many parts as each unit has small parts, and these, large and small, are in the same proportion. Used for the first time in *Construction*, this principle appears in nearly all my work (symmetrically or asymmetrically) until 1952."[2]

The 1980s dance public recently saw the young choreographer Douglas Wright present his dance *No Man Standing* to Cage's *Six Melodies for Violin and Piano* (1950), and the audience at the Bessie Schönberg Theater was able to recall the prealeatoric, pre-magnetic-tape Cage.[3] In the *Melodies*, Cage's durational rhythm allows a stepwise construction in the music—each intervallic shift held upon by the rhythmic controls—so that the listener is made aware of the monophony (these really are melodies) and of the shifting sense of time frames through which the components are viewed. As the music slowly accumulates in its unveiling, a series of overlapping "dissolves" in the listener's perception of the musical form continually frames the components in new ways. Each temporal unit is thus filled regularly and variously through the structural imbrication. The music has a drama both in the immediate, moment-by-moment response to such local configurations and in the listener's growing sense that more discoveries are to come—the present lack of knowledge about overall shape forces a suspension of conventional musical appetites in light of the accession to come. So dense, in fact, is the immediate sound-sense (the pressure of inspection allowed by monophony and by the restriction of violin and piano to twenty-three tones) that the listener's need for release from the musical logic leads to the mind's imposition of the structural frames as though by mental reflex: such involuntary perception of local and accumulated shape offers a promise of freedom from immediate pressure toward the system's anticipated self-disposal.

It was during the early 1940s that Cage and Cunningham began their collaboration. (Their first piece—*Credo in Us*—was presented in 1942). In 1944, Cunningham devised a dance, *Tossed as it is Untroubled*, whose choreography is said to have followed Cage's proportionally arranged musical structure. (In other collaborative works, Cage followed Cunningham's lead.) Cage's compositional technique (like Arnold Schoenberg's) freed his music from any structural dependence on a harmonic system, and it may have represented a general attempt by Cage to strengthen the rhythmic component in advanced music making at that time. The sound of such music has a "primitivistic" feel about it similar to qualities in the music of Erik Satie and George Antheil. The very title of *First Construction (in Metal)* suggests constructivist forebears—that is, a style simultaneously primitive (in the steady, quantitative outlay of information) and sophisticated (in the manner by which constituent units are manipulated to "free" the sound or to contrast macro- and micro-layers of rhythmic information).

As late as 1955, in his essay "Experimental Music," Cage continued to see the basis of musical rhythm as a matter of duration: "Rhythm is duration of any length coexisting in any states of succession and synchronicity."[4] I have never encountered a published discussion of Cunningham that has suggested that Cage's approach to musical rhythm may have been influential in any specific, technical sense on the formation of the choreographer's dance rhythm. (Possibly this is because the whole subject of the relationship between musical and dance rhythm is relatively unexplored. The two are not necessarily the same.) Neither am I privy to Cunningham's specific compositional techniques. (Cunningham has stated in interviews that music and dance share only one element—time— and that all other correspondences between the two arts are "intellectual" constructs.) But I suspect that the durational emphasis in Cage's composition of music may have its equivalent in Cunningham's dancemaking.

Indeed, there may have been a period influence on both Cage and Cunningham. The swing music of the thirties brought about a new appreciation of Bach's musical rhythm. Virgil Thomson has characterized swing rhythm as "quantitative."[5] Borrowing the term from prosody, Thomson has contrasted music that is accentual in its organization (including much popular dance music) with music that is organized according to "a unit of length." For Thomson, both big-band swing and a "Brandenburg" concerto are examples of quantitative rhythm, metrical units made up of lengths or durations of musical sound. Accentual music thus becomes "beat" music. Quantitative music de-emphasizes beat; it floats, it shimmers, it burnishes; it stickily and sweetly "jams." According to Thomson, much of the freedom of improvisational jazz is made possible by an unexpressed, steady, underlying quantitative rhythm. The durational values are hinted at in the musical decoration—anticipated, traced, or brushed in, allowed to hover through the percussive strokes of drum, cymbals, or double bass—providing impetus and ground rather than offering that immediate, multilayered play of pulse and pattern to be found in music based on an accentual rhythm. I suggest that John Cage's attempt to structure his rhythms according to a durational principle may have been his contribution to this area of musical discourse during the thirties and forties.

Listeners can recognize the decoration of a Bach concerto or the drive of a jam session. Cage's durational music features a similar free flotation and steady state; it is a music of powerlessness in power, of passivity achieved out of organized activity, of contrasting movement and stasis. In the 1950 *Melodies*, the aural weight builds up a chastened version of baroque or swing momentum. Each unit is under such immediate compositional pressure, such availability for the closest inspection, one would think that all impetus would die, fragment, evaporate. (And in some late 1940s musics, Cage investigated just such effects.) Which is to say that the durational element is substantive in Cage's work, and that this value may have its general relation to what Thomson has described as a "quantitative" rhythm.

The reason that I find the evidence of a mutual interest on the part of Cage and Cunningham in this aspect of rhythm to be of use when watching the choreographer's works is that otherwise I know of no other way to explain the particular experience of Cunningham rhythm—its weight, its inclusiveness, its environment. Any dancer brought up through traditional classroom training in ballet, tap, flamenco, etc., knows that there is something special and enveloping about the Cunningham metric. Whether the educated member of the audience finds that metric liberating or claustrophobic is a matter of taste, education, or prejudice. But I think that something like the quality I am describing is identifiable in Cunningham's dance.

Such a view would explain certain enduring and characteristic features of his style. For example, simply to say that Cunningham's dances have an extraordinary command of large-scale rhythmic strategies is to say very little. Those big proportions are obviously not arrived at after the fact; they are not in any simple sense an inheritance from Martha Graham's commodious idea of theatrical time; they are not applied from "outside"; and they are not in any simple sense macro-versions of smaller dance units. It is as though Cunningham had found a method to de-emphasize any conventional "accentual" dance components in his work (except for purposes of satire or allusion). By working for durational qualities, Cunningham may have derived a method for avoiding all the clichés of conventional dance, all the encrusted "accentual" patterns that have grown up around dance forms—folk, theatrical, balletic. Freshness in dance material is thus forced by Cunningham through a singular approach to compositional method. Perhaps this also explains why some audiences and dancers—trained by dance styles formed out of a residue of accentual dance rhythms—experience an initial difficulty adjusting to the Cunningham metric.

It would also explain why a production like American Ballet Theatre's *Duets* proves inadequate. If Cunningham's dance rhythm possesses a strong durational element, then certain seductive charms of his dance classicism would be vulnerable to misinterpretation by ballet executants. For example, I suspect that, for Cunningham, *plastique* is merely one more means of "filling" the dance duration; *plastique* does not have the substantive powers of rhythmic extension that it has in ballet. At best it would work—like Bach's harmony and counterpoint—to hold attention *through* the metrical unit. It is guide rather than destination. (Actually, the choreography of Petipa, Bournonville, and Balanchine at times also exploits that kind of plastic guidance.) Cunningham works regularly to control *plastique*, to de-emphasize inherited ideas about sculptural values in dance, and to use his version of such values to concentrate and expose the underlying rhythmic idea. He allows his best performers to generate additional layers of rhythmic information over his material, to thicken the mixture, whereas in classical ballet the choreographer readily accommodates such layerings, builds them in. Those of us in the ballet crowd can—these days, must—take our pleasures where we find them. But the fan of both ballet and Cunningham makes allowances for the stylistic differences involved. Only an ABT can afford to level them. Cunningham asks his followers to watch all dance objectively. In that sense, the ABT production hadn't a Cagean chance. Not only does the version say little about Cunningham; it does little for the training of the ABT dancers—except postpone balletic choices of real stylistic consequence.

Seen in this way, Cunningham's percussive dance patterns—his variations upon his dance themes—would be the choreographer's free "improvisation" over the rhythmic ground, as in Bach and swing. (The improvisation is a compositional achievement rather than a performance choice.) Cunningham would thus purchase the freedom for brilliant "baroque" variations from the discipline of the durational control. As in those forms of modern music where harmony and counterpoint no longer dictate matters of rhythmic structure, Cunningham's *plastique* and local accent are deliberately subjugated to the controls of his dance rhythm.

This may be why my dancer friends claim they can "count" Cunningham. The durational lengths are something like an unexpressed, expanded ostinato beneath the dance phrases; they may even help beginning Cunningham dancers learn to orient themselves in a form of dance so independent of conventional musical "counts." (The question would be, what are Cunningham's dancers counting? Accentual patterns? Time lengths?) Indeed, the educated response in any viewing audience would be to locate a pulse beneath such dancing, especially when its phrasal elements are irregular and unpredictable. In *Rebus* (1975) or *Torse* (1976), Cunningham stretches the boundaries of a dance dynamics and sustained allegro invention: the experiment locates the viewer's sense of durational rhythm around the borders of its possible sustainment, and the dance rhythm—forced and highlighted—acquires a quality of an amplified "beat" such as is found in certain forms of music that are obviously accentual in their organization. Perhaps this is one reason why so many of Cunningham's postmodern followers have used varieties of "pulse" music (both yesterday's swing and today's "pulse" exploit a motoric rhythm). In interpreting the master, in updating him for the eighties, the postmoderns often parody Cunningham's durational rhythms, turning them into inflated accentual ones, as rock music in the fifties simplified and exaggerated the accentual components of popular jazz dance rhythms in pursuit of the big beat. Today's postmoderns glance at Cunningham's rhythms, hear-tell of a metrical process, and then mass-produce in their own work the squarest possible dance phrasing under the banner of a theoretical triumph.

The best recent Cunningham dances (*Landrover* [1972], *Sounddance* [1975], *Solo* [1975], *Fractions* [1977], *Quartet* [1982], *Phrases* [1984]) would resemble Bach or swing on one level: they so advertise their freedom from the underlying metrical ground that we are tantalized into trying to locate any "beat" at such heady distance. Once Cunningham had enunciated his approach to dance rhythm, any other dance project that evidenced a compositional reliance on the inheritance of accentual rhythmic ideas—a tradition of impulses and formal guides that had always sustained and educated choreographers in conventional dance styles—would be seen by Cunningham and his followers as marked by facility, by a lack of proper and rigorous investigation of dance basics. Accentual rhythm in a dance equaled conventionality. Durational rhythm became the post-fifties avant-garde given (as it was for Nijinsky in *L'Après-midi d'un faune*).

A conventional choreographer—by that I mean one who assumes that the unconventional component of dance is self-evident—lives rather easily with the accentual residue of the past. He observes it, absorbs it, reconstitutes it. And a traditionalist like George Balanchine sometimes joins a durational metric to his primarily accentual one: an example would be the play with tempi and deaccelerando devices in his choreography to Hindemith's *Kammermusik No. 2*. Again, the interplay of accentual dance rhythm and durational musical accompaniment in Balanchine's *Concerto Barocco* is one source of that ballet's continuing challenge to performers. (Among other things, Balanchine used the big-band link with Bach to highlight that area of female adagio technique that is quasi-durational in its rhythm.) An unconventional choreographer like Merce Cunningham, on the other hand, suspects the residues of accentual dance rhythm to the extent of devising a method of self-protection against them. There is a sense in which Cunningham's defensiveness toward the matter of traditional dance may represent a last gasp of nineteenth-century vitalism, with its emphasis upon the purification of the spirit via radical disciplinary means. If so, Cunningham may not have purged his work of a "vitalistic" element as completely as Marcel Duchamp's antivitalist esthetic requires.

Many of the "radicalisms" used to characterize Cunningham's dance are subservient to this use of durational rhythmic values. The fractured, evenly exposed, "elemental" dance components signal their integrity—their service to a temporal control. An aesthetic of assemblage (facets organized within a field) works ironically to throw attention onto the original "free" selection of materials. (Such freedom is restated in the absence of traditional stage focus or hierarchical stage patterns.) The neutral (because geometrically simplified) *plastique* of the dancers serves to carry primary rhythmic information and to frame the rhythmic content. The *allegro* phrases and long-held groupings in Cunningham's style trace durational measures. The variety of movement components (*any* movement—found, indeterminate, chance-derived—can serve as dance material) permits the eye choice—and allows the choreographer to dramatize the distance he can place between surface decoration and rhythmic ground. The dancers interpret their assigned material for the audience, adding to the mix their inevitably more "conventionalized" versions of Cunningham's unconventional dance ideas. The dancer's virtuosity must therefore be an "intellectual" one. The dance material is held in evidently raw form long enough so that the choreographer can work quasi-musical processes of manipulation (canon, retrograde, inversion, etc.) upon it and so the evidence of those processes can be partially seen, thus adding the pleasure of analysis to the display, the audience recognizing the basic materials but glimpsing their preparation prior to final compositional shaping.

All of these categories of innovation are minor matters, of course, in comparison to other, more substantive areas of dance opened up by a durational approach to rhythm: qualities of attack, preparation, transition, phrasing, etc. In fact, it is easier to give credence to the presence of something like a durational rhythm in Cunningham's dance than to the claim for a general "baroque" esthetic of developmental variation. If it is true, for example, that Cunningham works free variations on his dance themes, what is fascinating is the nature of those themes; the resultant floridity in the dance facture would be on an inevitably lower level of interest. In fact, if there is a theme-and-variation process going on, what does it consist of? In other words, what are Cunningham's dance equivalents of music's harmonic and contrapuntal devices? Does his dance *plastique* really read as such a device, as I have suggested it may? Is it possible that Cunningham's idea of variation technique only "turns the ground"—allowing another process of variation to occur in performance? If so, what are the conditions of Cunningham performance that allow a further analysis? Such questions do not have easy answers, but they identify living areas of Cunningham's dance thought in a way that restatements of the publicized Cunningham-Cage general esthetic no longer do. If Cunningham's dances "develop"—generate themselves from within—in ways that are different from the dances of other choreographers, I suspect the difference may derive from an approach as basic as Cunningham's durational rhythm.

All the usual critical and theoretical approaches to Cunningham's dance don't really carry us very far. If we admit the presence of a durational emphasis in Cunningham's dance rhythm, however, some things can be said. The Cunningham dancer must confront certain challenges. The dancers must generally "hide" the initiation that gets them into a dance phrase, much as dancers trained in ballet must cover their preparation. I suspect this is Cunningham's way of fighting the complacency that a durational approach to rhythm could precipitate. The performer must negotiate the long and short lengths in the dance rhythm, using the persistence of the durational units and the allowed extent of Cunningham's (often discontinuous) phrases. The metrical lengths thus expose a dancer to immediate challenges that accentual rhythms do not. The phrases require a light, tensionless hand to keep them transparent, while the dancer simultaneously profiles and inflects them, even in their sometime brevity. The Cunningham phrase has these features: it expands outward from within, floated by the durational quantities; and it is pressured toward succinct statement from without because of the self-consciously "structural" emphasis. The dancers must avoid both complacency and busywork. They cannot "ride" the indications of an accentual dance rhythm as ballet or tap dancers can. They choose actively. An accentual dance rhythm allows the performer to pick from among arranged highlights. The durational approach of Cunningham forces regularity of choice, and the soloists' accents seem their own in their performance weight. The danger in performing Cunningham is that the dancers may project an overwilled, premeditated lifelessness. The accentual approach, on the other hand, makes spontaneity crucial, and its danger for the performer is mindless joyriding.

In the Events context of presentation, Cunningham's dance materials must stand up to any variety of sound matrices thrown at them. When excerpts from several works in the current Cunningham repertory are olioed across the length of an Event, the durational rhythm presents nary a jarring splice between works of very different technical requirements and atmospheres. An Event is a sign on a large scale that Cunningham's dance rhythm has a weight, a momentum, and an homogeneity. The juxtaposition of excerpts from several works sometimes allows an Event more contrast within an evening than individual Cunningham works sometimes offer, between one another and within themselves. When this happens, I think it is because of Cunningham's tenacity in holding to his rhythmic approach.

There is a paradox in a dance esthetic that asks us to concentrate *only* on the surface of the spectacle while simultaneously exploiting a tension between an underlying organizational principle and the richly elaborated surface. One reason commentators seize on a "baroque" approach to Cunningham is that the idea posits a prior identification of thematic material while converting the dance surface into so much brilliant ornamentation or choreographic improvisation. It is possible that Cunningham's actual thematic materials require a less complacent approach for their identification, and that the progress of his dance conducts itself—sustains itself—in a fashion that goes beyond conventional ideas of variation technique. Not only is it difficult to extend the "baroque" analogy from the musical and plastic arts to Cunningham's dance style without falling into a critical impression, but the attempt reminds us of the very different matrix from which Cage and Cunningham derive their thematic materials.[6] For example, Cage conceives of musical duration in an absolutely temporal sense; in contrast, Virgil Thomson conceives of a "quantitative" metric as in complicity with a received musical tradition. Cunningham may insist upon his choreographic absolutes as well, and such an insistence renders thematic identification in his dances a challenge for critical analysis. The idea of a "baroque" esthetic requires that thematic materials be precisely identified. An analyst of dance rhythm—Kenneth King, for example—could make a catalog of Cunningham's durational metric values and his characteristic surface formulas for elaboration. Such an approach would have definite interest. But I'm not sure that such an analysis is more than a beginning.

Early Cunningham gained some of its initial shock from confronting the audience with the durational approach. As patterns and formulas in his repertory accumulated, the surface of Cunningham dance gained in its ability to guide the performer and the viewer in the perception of the rhythmical ideas, and that surface has at length acquired a quasi-accentual aspect. Early Cunningham dancers could appear innovative from the "perversity" of an "antidance" (because anti-accentual) approach. The later Cunningham dancers join a developed metrical idiom, so they must reinvent for the new audience something like that original shock. Today's dancers must first sustain their phrase length, then create as thickly encrusted and detailed a surface profile as they can, while never abandoning their obligation to reassert the deeper controls of durational periods. The dancers must navigate between surface and ground. In this sense, time and change have themselves allowed one level in Cunningham's dance that might be described as "baroque." In *Torse* and *Rebus,* the original cast performed full-out on the heavily stressed surface patterns; there was no time to play them off against the durational ground. The result was as close as Cunningham has come to bombast.

This play of surface and ground may be the best (because overriding) example in Cunningham's style of what French estheticians on the left like to think of as his nonhierarchical, "open," expository achievement—in which both foreground and background, and, indeed, all framing devices, are confessed as distinct and nonillusionary tools, and each compositional element is used as just one more auxiliary (and thus uncoercive) control. Indeed, a durational rhythm itself would serve—in its implications—as a framing device, a principal background for exquisitely chosen choreographic elements. But a rhythm is a useful tool for a dancemaker only in its hold on his imagination, and a good new Cunningham dance is a world of hierarchical movement discriminations. *Phrases* (1984; New York premiere March 5, 1985), his best new piece since *Fractions* (1977–78), reminds us of what Cunningham basics are meant to accomplish. *Phrases* has all the weight we expect in Cunningham's temporal world. It's a fully stated piece, unlike *Native Green* (1985) and *Doubles* (1984), which clip their feathers close. *Phrases* thus has time to unfurl a range of "structural" bracketings, types of rhythmic organization. The largesse of invention begs the question of an easy tag—"baroque" doesn't quite fit. And the durational approach gives us again the sometime pathos of the Cunningham spectacle, the dancers' details absorbed, swallowed in the context, and yet regularly, almost defiantly, reiterated. *Phrases* is an update of one of those ensemble works of the seventies—*Landrover, Rebus, Torse*—but warmed and individualized. The choreographer himself visits his creatures in one of those cameo roles he makes for himself, the ghostly super of the co-op. David Bradshaw's costumes head toward basic blacks and whites and then veer toward the original ochres just before the end. And Cunningham has arranged one of his surefire endings—the stage darkening and swept by vigilant patrols.

But the dance details are fresh and almost impossible to categorize as one watches. Their play is too agile and their deployment too flexed. The dance figures—reversed, echoed, refracted, time-delayed—question the eyes' ability to bracket a "phrase." Thus, we look even more closely, only to discover the parodic elements within the bracketings: for example, the quoted *balancés* of Cunningham and Cathy Kerr during their *entrée*. The quotes are yet another fantastication, a witty reference this time to classical ideas of phrasing.

The overlapped bracketings force our gaze within and without simultaneously. Without: to that extraordinary mixture of quotidian gesture with heroic image everywhere in Cunningham, as, for example, in Robert Swinston's winged entrance across the back of the stage with three attendant women, or Chris Komar's and Karen Fink's *pas de bourrée* progress across the back with changing arm positions. Within: the accentual surprises and virtuoso initiations, as in Swinston's pivot leaps when he first appears in white or in Alan Good's jumps just before he is joined by Kerr toward the end. It is this double vision that permits Cunningham his boldest ploys—surprising interruptions and resumptions of his line of thought.

In *Phrases*, the line is both finer and larger than any one of its signs. The durational rhythm is part of the *bas relief* of the Cunningham style: it aids in the release of the dance details even as it holds them. Thus, embellishment itself becomes context. We sense that the dance idea's full statement is withheld so as not to overapproximate its locus. The individual vibrato of the piece (an aural effect, as well as visual, given the percussiveness of the Cunningham style) pulls us in. *Phrases* has the characteristics of all of Cunningham's best work: a natural calm, an acclimated alertness, a deepening of rhythmic thought, and a resultant iridescence.

Phrases escapes the principal danger in a durational metric from a compositional point of view—a "materialism" of dance facture, a lack of skepticism toward the produced surface of the dance. For example, ballet choreographers who employ a durational component in their work—I am thinking of Jerome Robbins and Eliot Feld—sometimes allow their materials to harden into phrasal units intractable to variation or regeneration. Cunningham, on the other hand, maintains a critical attitude toward the durational metric. His dance, as in *Phrases,* is something more than an illustration of methodology or a certification of craft. The surface of his dance is often closer to a balletic surface than is the work of many "classical" choreographers. Perhaps this explains American Ballet Theatre's fascination with that surface.

Cunningham's durational dance rhythm suggests a more methodical, strategically held esthetic than can be usefully admitted by those who advertise Cunningham dance. Actually, I suspect that Cunningham's conception of dance rhythm is a means whereby he can subject his materials to regular observation, to inspection—i.e., that it is a precompositional laboratory technique out of which the specifics of individual works are allowed to develop. The master's secret is less in his use of a type of rhythm than in the quality of his inspection of materials. The other reason that apologists for the Cunningham style may not have found it useful to discuss this aspect of Cunningham's dance is that a theory of his rhythm would posit a dependence on musical sources and analogies (Bach, swing, Cage) that would be at variance with Cunningham's stated goal of making dance independent of all such immediate and "authoritarian" controls. To suggest that durational or quantitative rhythm is at the base of the Cunningham esthetic makes the master seem subject to the laws of fashion in the arts (for example, the same laws that linked up the Bach revival around 1900 with the primitivistic experiments of Picasso and Nijinsky, that early conjunction of experimental tastes in advance of the thirties' back-to-Bach movement). After all, the Duchampian esthetic of Cage and Cunningham is supposed to exist outside of history, beyond strict influence and any fashion. Merce of Egypt, indeed. But a thinking audience may have to risk that kind of misprision in order to rescue Cunningham from the boutique sensibility of the eighties.

From the evidence of its influence, Cunningham's durational orientation appeals to today's neophyte choreographer as sheer availability, dance matter conveniently cleansed of ostentatious stylistic reference, solid enough to cry out for shaping, roomy enough to allow for performance choices freed from conventional ideas of formula or drama. For the young, the style is risky business for fun and profit. In its most profligate examples, Cunningham's extended academy (all those choreographers who have danced with his company and then left to choreograph, and all those choreographers—many more—who borrow ideas from his example) is capable of producing just as much second-rate dance as any other school; but the antisentimentality of Cunningham's method helps accustom young choreographers to their own way of moving. What is then done with the discovered individuality is dependent on choices that the young must manage beyond the help of any master. The elements of Cunningham's style trigger free-thinking dancers and galvanize potential dancemakers. The approach does not guarantee anything beyond such instigation.

Graduates of the Cunningham academy cover the earth, and the colonialization has partially come about because of the concentration in Cunningham's recent works on ensemble over soloist roles. Dancers come into the company, stay for a year or two, and then graduate to form companies of their own around the globe. In Cunningham's current company, the relationship of soloist to ensemble is discussed only intermittently in new additions to the repertory, and often with the choreographer taking the solo roles. Dancers seldom "move up"; there is no "up" in the avant-garde. But they may not also in any observable sense become more *themselves* in interesting and new ways as we watch them season after season. (That this situation exists within companies—Tharp's is another one—which claim a "radical" esthetic and which presumably attempt a regular radical redefinition of concepts like "role" and "characterization" is something of a paradox.) A dance experimentalist can devote decades to an ensemble style and the examination of its "impersonal" energies without ever attaining that higher impersonality that regularly produces soloists. As a result, ambitious dancers in such companies eventually strike out on their own and make "radical" dances for themselves, spawning yet another generation of dance makers. (Modern-dance history reads like self-preservation by other means.) In this way, too, Cunningham's approach to dance rhythm has become an aspect of dance language propagated throughout the West.

Notes

1. Quoted in Paul Griffiths, *Cage* (New York: Oxford University Press, 1981), 11.
2. John Cage, Notes on *First Construction (in Metal)* (1934), in the album booklet for George Avakian's recording *The 25-Year Retrospective Concert of the Music of John Cage*, recorded in performance at Town Hall, New York, 15 May 1958. (The 1959 album has recently been reissued.)
3. In a 1950 review, Virgil Thomson described Cage's structural rhythm this way: "John Cage employs a numerical ratio in any piece between the phrase, the period, and the whole, the phrase occupying a time measure which is the square root of the whole time and the periods occupying times proportional to those of the different rhythmic motifs within the phrase. This procedure, though it allows for asymmetry within the phrase and period, produces a

tight symmetry in the whole composition. . . ." Quoted from "Atonality Today," originally published in the *New York Herald Tribune,* 5 February 1950; reprinted in *A Virgil Thomson Reader* (New York: E.P. Dutton, 1981), 340.

4. John Cage, "Experimental Music," *The Score and I.M.A. Magazine,* 12 (June 1955): 65–68. Reprinted in John Cage, *Silence: Lectures and Writings by John Cage* (Middletown, CT: Wesleyan University Press, 1973), 15.

5. See "Swing Music" and "Swing Again" in Virgil Thomson, *A Virgil Thomson Reader* (New York: E.P. Dutton, 1981), 28–32 and 33–37. The essays were first published in *Modern Music* in 1936 and 1938.

6. See Earle Brown's comments on "proportional" or "nonmetric" musical notation in relation to Cunningham's dance, in "The Forming of an Aesthetic: Merce Cunningham and John Cage," *Ballet Review,* XIII/3 (Fall 1985). Brown's Cunningham pioneers a metrically unconventional or nonmetrical rhythm. From that perspective, my analysis (which sees Cunningham's dance rhythm resolving itself into durational periods beyond whatever "unconventionality" it attains) would be retardative.

Alastair Macaulay

THE MERCE EXPERIENCE (1988)

The story is told that an eminent figure in the dance world recently wrote to Merce Cunningham politely asking him to send, for reference purposes, a brief résumé of what he had done "since leaving Martha." Well, Cunningham left the Martha Graham company in 1945. This summer will mark thirty-five years of his own company's existence—over half his life. This (and much more) is history—isn't it?

In March, Cunningham presented at the Joyce Theatre the longest season of repertory he has ever given in New York: seven performances a week, four weeks, thirteen works. This is the most sustained exposure to his work that any city has had since that surprising season in London in 1964, when a week's visit was so warmly acclaimed that it was turned into a month's stay.

Twenty-four years later, a month of Merce no longer provokes astonished hosannas or outraged jeers. He is simply a landmark. Has something been lost in the process? No doubt. I never saw Carolyn Brown, Viola Farber, or other Cunningham dancers of that generation perform onstage, and I'm prepared to accept that, with their departure, a certain greatness vanished from the face of the world—just as I do when thinking of other dancers I never saw, like Violette Verdy and Edward Villella. And it is possible, I suppose, to see the revivals of *RainForest* (1968) and *Septet* (1953) mainly as ghost-town ballets. But Cunningham's recent repertory is no decaying museum or academic exercise ground, and his dancers aren't machines or clones. Far from it. Technique in Cunningham performance today is highly accomplished, and almost every iota of it is dissolved into style. Each of the men has registered as a character for

173

some time; in recent seasons, the women have begun to follow suit, although some of them some of the time still like to maintain a good-girl impersonality. A few newcomers in the past couple of years, such as Dennis O'Connor and Larissa McGoldrick, have at once made an explosive, eccentric impact on the repertory; and the newest girl, Kimberly Bartosik, dances as if her whole life had been invested in joining this company. Experienced performers like Alan Good, Robert Swinston, Victoria Finlayson, and Kristy Santimyer project their own imaginative spell in all they do.

So when at other performances in March several New York dancegoers told me without any very good reason that they "didn't make it to Merce this season," I was stumped. ("I can't stand him" would have been reason enough.) Even in a city with the dance abundance of New York, a month of this repertory is too rich to be overlooked. What greater choreographers are active today? And what choreographer is in finer harmony with his present gathering of dancers?

During the eighties, it is time to say, Cunningham's choreography has shown a fresh, autumnal wisdom—whether tragic (*Quartet* [1982]), idyllic (*Pictures* [1984]), lyrical (*Doubles* [1984]), bleak (*Shards* [1987]), or all these things by turns (*Fabrications* [1987]). It would be wrong to assume that just because Cunningham is no longer a revolutionary his work has had its day. Actually, most years of this decade have given us at least one new masterpiece; 1987, for instance, produced *Shards*, *Fabrications*, and the stage version of *Points in Space*. By such standards, 1988's new items—*Eleven*, in its world premiere; *Carousal* (1987), new to New York; the *RainForest* revival—should make the Joyce weeks rank as small beer. True, *RainForest* is part of Cunningham's legend (even if its most famed component is its Warhol decor: the billowing array of helium-filled silver pillows—they're both floating foliage and swaying undergrowth). It's still an arrestingly conceived work, its dances constructed largely of nonacademic material and marked by a subdued, feral quality. At the opening-night performance, it struck me as more subdued than feral—undernuanced. Even those pillows were well behaved. Not surprisingly, the revival elicited murmurs of nostalgia: "Helium isn't what it was when we were what we were," and so on. As for the premieres, *Carousal* was a patchwork of convivial episodes; incidentally fascinating, it was flimsy over all. *Eleven*, which contained variations on the choreographic forms Cunningham has been employing in recent years, and which in other circumstances might have emerged as an elegant work, was crippled by its score and its costumes.

And yet it was an enthralling season. The Merce experience remains—the Merce experience, that is, as it has come to be in the mid-eighties. The greatest pleasure of these seasons lies not in the premieres or the golden oldies but in one's gradual immersion in those dancers, those dances, and those things which run deepest in his work: the unique stillnesses and distances and perspectives onstage; the odd, flat, natural rhythms; the countless resonances and ambiguities of each piece.

The finest Merce experience I have ever had was in Montreal in 1985, with a triple bill of *Inlets 2* (1983), *Doubles*, and *Pictures*. Yes, three idylls: it was like going from the countryside of Bohemia to the Forest of Arden and then on to Prospero's isle. No other choreographer in history could have brought it off. All three works were to be seen at the Joyce this year, albeit on different programs. In *Inlets 2*, one of Cunningham's most hushed nature studies, I cherish the long-held Seurat poses in profile, the echoes of Nijinsky's *Faune* choreography they suggest, and the way they realize Edwin Denby's point about *Faune* that "the space between the figures becomes a firm body of air, a lucid statement of relationship, in the way intervening space does in the modern academy of Cézanne, Seurat, and Picasso." Above all, the work shows how those flat rhythms of Cunningham dance can catch the very essence of animal life: I see birds floating, taking wing, hovering, resettling; rodents scuttling and then freezing. This evocation of fauna, which Cunningham can reinforce in some dances with unspecific pictorial suggestions (hands held like paws, as in *RainForest*; the curve of a back; the angle of a haunch; the arch of a neck), is achieved primarily through timing. And it is part of his poetic genius that he can convey all this while employing in other works the most purely academic vocabulary. In *Points in Space* an ensemble of women, all facing the same way to concentrate on the rigors of stationary adagio, will suddenly change tempo and travel across the stage: something has disturbed this flock. In *Doubles* there is a web of rhythm: it is the most lyrically buoyant work in the repertory. The two women who walk around the stage's perimeter for long spells, and off into the wings and on again as if they'd never been absent, are all tender, quiet, calm legato. The other dancers have a much wider range of accent, and the solos appear peacefully full of human self-contradictions. *Pictures*, with its miraculous tableaux of dancers linked in horizontal lines, its many serene slow variations on walking, presents dancers in an unaffected, rapt state of grace. Each dancer establishes a single tempo upon entrance and maintains it for a long span of time.

Some Cunningham works seem deliberately to splice material from two or more others. *Shards* grafts the stillnesses and concentration of *Inlets 2* onto the racked, dark urgency of *Quartet*. What seems at first to be a nature study is punctuated by contained violence. Tension builds. No one communicates. *Fabrications* evokes phrases and motifs from numerous other works from the repertory, past and present, and assembles them into a broad canvas unlike anything else this choreographer has made.

There are many things in Cunningham's work that have long reminded me of Chekhov: the poignant overlap of several different narrative threads, the variety of material within any one character's solo, the contrast of fluent lyricism and blunt prosiness as a natural condition of human existence. *Fabrications* is his most thoroughly Chekhovian work, and it is like another Chekhovian dance work, by Frederick Ashton: it's Merce's *Enigma Variations*—

rich in brief, telling incidents and in dramatic ironies. The work is studded with short duets in which couple after couple demonstrate their own species of cooperation and mutual absorption. Each duet counts powerfully, and even more moving is the way the duets are set apart from the ensembles that are the work's basic orchestration. Toward the end, Cunningham brings six couples on together in a ring, all performing the same few charged phrases of supported adagio. But there is no sense of completion in this—partly because you can't quite forget the fleeting glimpses you've had of soloists distanced from the main action, among them that old man who has bumbled from time to time across the stage. The score, by Emanuel Dimas de Melo Pimenta, seems to augment the fluctuations of feeling and immediacy in the work, and helps you to sense that this is one man's memory of a society and intimacies gone by.

In no other choreographer's repertory is stasis so expressive. Dancers standing still, dancers maintaining cool balance without a tremor, tableaux of stationary dancers supported or unsupported: these are basic Cunningham fare, and *Septet* reveals that they have been since at least 1953. In a central passage of this work, we see a row of three male-female couples. As the Satie music proceeds, each woman hangs on her partner, and each is motionless in a different bleak pose: individual urgency preserved in amber. Cunningham went on to invent variations on this theme. How many straight lines, horizontal or diagonal, has he made out of three pairs, each carved in a different stationary position? And always the eye is rewarded as it takes in the geometrical intricacy and organizational wit of the tableau. But in the context of *Septet* the image has a peculiar force: it reminds me, curiously, less of other Cunningham works than of a dance for the two secondary couples late in Balanchine's Robert Schumann ballet, where each women rests or presses upon her partner in one still pose after another. In *Septet*, it reinforces the point of a note that Cunningham used to publish in the programs between 1955 and 1964—that the ballet's subject "is Eros," and its occurrence "is at the intersection of joy and sorrow." (Cunningham was right, however, not to use that note in the eighties revival. We can see now how very many things *Septet* is "about"—not least, ballet tradition and Merce's individual talent.)

Cunningham's work reminds me of many things just because it is about people dancing and because of its catholic notion of what dancing can include. Watching the delicious opening duet (or double solo) of *Carousal*, I recalled Denby's words about certain Balanchine ballets: "What an extraordinary absence of prejudice as to what is proper in classicism these odd works show." Chris Komar and Dennis O'Connor—left and right of center, respectively—execute two different solos that return at different points to the same motif, a very Cunningham pattern of high-plucked, treading footwork that gets them nowhere in particular. Doing it, they resemble wading birds, or Wilis in *Giselle*. But each solo contains what dance analysts would call "movement information" of a completely distinct kind. Sometimes the distinction is in a minor detail. Each man retreats into a striking fourth position, leans backward, chest spread proudly, and looks over his shoulder: it's angled so that whereas Komar looks away from us, tossing his head back, right out of sight, as if in despair, O'Connor turns his face to us with a touch of self-glamorizing nonchalance. What a neatly odd couple (Komar has been in the company fourteen years longer than O'Connor; both are blond and of a height), and what a neatly odd split-focus duet (O'Connor's section contains falls, rolls, and hops that are nothing like Komar's). If only *Carousal* were that *neatly* odd throughout. Instead, it's a list of communal vignettes that don't cohere. We never recapture the taut rhythm of the opening.

Eleven, of course, is a right little tease. After all, we knew where we were with *Septet*, which is for six dancers, and with *Quartet*, for five. But *Eleven* has *eleven* dancers, and occasionally they're all onstage together. The Master must mean *something* by this, but I missed it. Fending off the wretched music, as I tried to do at a second performance, I isolated several new aspects of movement information. In particular, the duets here are different. Throughout the eighties, Cunningham's duets have tended to follow the rules of ice dancing; no high lifts and not more than a yard or so between male and female. But here are couples addressing each other with the whole width of the stage between them, sometimes even along a diagonal bisected by another couple's duet. There are further points to admire, not least a rather Ashtonian trio for two men and a woman, in which Patricia Lent's line as she is lifted by Robert Swinston is echoed by the stationary Alan Good. But to what end? Robert Ashley's score is Cunningham's most intrusive to date. Two metrical monologues, chanted in contrasting Japanese and American accents, that turn out to be a dialogue of sorts taken from a scene in a post-mod, sci-fi soap opera, whose metres may at times be related to the choreography . . . And, yes, while I was trying not to listen, whole sections of Cunningham invention went in one eye and out the other.

Would that I could say the same of the designs. The company's design department has for almost four years been in the undistinguished hands of William Anastasi and Dove Bradshaw. At their undistinguished best (*Native Green* [1985], not seen this season; the videodance original of *Points in Space* [1986]; the *Shards* costumes), they seem to design with at least a backward glance at the more striking work of their predecessors. Thank heaven, there were no backdrops for *Carousal* or *Eleven*. The *Eleven* costumes, and the backdrops for *Grange Eve* (1986), *Fabrications*, and *Shards*, suggest little Abstract Expressionist sketches blown up and thrown onto the stage like custard pies. The baggy costumes used in *Fabrications*, *Grange Eve*, and *Carousal* are appropriate to those works' moods. Even so, all of them lack any theatrical dimension, and the specific characteristics of each are so unmemorable that the dancers seem to be dressed in rehearsal kit, waiting until the next Mark Lancaster comes along to array them in impeccable combinations of Cézanne colors.

It is still an unwritten law of Cunningham dance theatre that he, in his very late sixties, should appear in one work per evening. And the works he uses for this purpose—*Quartet, Pictures, Grange Eve, Fabrications*—compose a repertory. To enjoy watching him is to enjoy the pleasure of ruins—the way we enjoy the artistry of those singers who committed their singing to the earliest 78s when they were long past their vocal prime. It would be courteous to say, as Herman Klein said of Adelina Patti's recordings, that you are observing the *beaux restes* of great singing, but, really, Cunningham's aren't very *beaux*. And there isn't a lot left he can do. Few things are simpler for a dancer than to rise from a kneeling position. When Cunningham does it in *Fabrications*, however, he steadies himself with one hand during the first part of the maneuver. Yet he does it with exactly the same timing at every performance. The precise spontaneity is endearing. It reminds me of Ralph Richardson's performance, at a similar age, in a William Douglas Home play I have otherwise forgotten, in which he made something touchingly hilarious out of slowly bending his knees and solemnly preparing to sit on a lawn. Cunningham is growing old—publicly, ungracefully, disarmingly.

Nancy Dalva

THE WAY OF MERCE (1992)

"Chance is the dogma, but look deeper."

Carolyn Brown[1]

". . . if the dancer dances, *everything is there. The meaning is there if that's what you want."*

Merce Cunningham[2]

Starting nearly fifty years ago, Merce Cunningham began to change the way people dance and the way people see dancing in the same way that Picasso and the cubists changed the way people painted and the way people saw painting.

He took dance apart and put it back together again, leaving out all but the most essential. He stripped dance of conventional narrative; he ordered it by chance procedures; he conceived it without music and without decor. He took it out of the proscenium (but later put it back) and exploded the stage picture into fragments. He made the viewer the *auteur*. The great irony of all this is that only a great storyteller possessed of extraordinary intrinsic musicality could have stripped away so much and be left with more. Cunningham is able to separate dance from its traditional trappings not because dance does not need them, but because dance—at least in his hands—already has them.

There has been a lot said about Merce Cunningham and John Cage and their working method—most of it said by neither of them. But of all of the odd things people have thought about Cunningham's dances over the years, the oddest—including the notion that the dances are in part or whole improvisational—have arisen from his use of chance, the most confusing element of the easiest place to see Cunningham rhythm is his unison sections, and the easiest place to find such sections is in the early video works choreographed first for camera, then transferred to the stage. Here one finds the dancers disposed in squads. To see one squad opposed against another is to see two unisons at once: basic Cunningham counterpoint.

Always—in stage, on film, in videos, and in rehearsal—the dancers seem to be dancing *to* something—keeping up with it, slowing down to it—their phrasing exquisite and driven. By what? By the sound—or the memory—of Cunningham's own snapping and clapping. Merce Cunningham works with a stopwatch. He is the White Rabbit ("I'm late! I'm late!") of choreographers, and in his own way the most musical of all. One could see this when he revived *Septet*, made in 1953 to Erik Satie's *Trois Morceaux en Forme de Poire*. To see *Septet* is to realize that, for Cunningham, working to music must be like turning on the radio when the record player is already on. It interferes with music he already hears.

Using a plot would interfere with Cunningham's storytelling in a similar way. It is here that the dogma is most pernicious: that the dances have no obvious narratives or superimposed mood has led to the notion that they tell no stories. Further, this lack of invented roles and moods has led some viewers to find the performers impersonal. The exact opposite is true. The work is in fact personality-driven, for what could be more personal, more transparent, than dancers who are always performing as themselves? Cunningham himself has said:

> The idea of personality not being there isn't true simply because when the dancers do it, they in doing it take it on—it's like a second skin.

If there has been a general trend in Cunningham criticism in the last decade, it has in fact been a movement away from calling the dances "abstract." Today, the critically correct position is to call them "dramatic," in recognition of their inherent theatricality. Cunningham himself, in conversation about his work, often talks about "the theater"[8] instead of "the dance." Generally speaking, when people write about the dramatic aspect of these dances, they are referring either to the actorly aspect of Cunningham's own performances, or to the overall tone of a piece—its lightness, or darkness. As Noël Carroll and Sally Banes wrote in 1983 in *Ballet Review*, "We don't paraphrase his dances into propositions about the nature of art . . . nor do we take them to be alchemical allegories."[9]

Maybe not, but there is nothing in the dances that deters this. Actually, Cunningham himself looks more and more woolly and wizardly every year. Where he used to look like Prospero, he now looks like Lear or, in his lighthearted moments, a sort of dotty Merlin. Of all the choreographers who have taken to the American stage, he's the one who'd look right at home with an owl on his shoulder. In the current repertory, the dances in which he performs lend themselves the most easily to story telling. They are also instantly dramatic: the contrast between Cunningham and his company is a bold one.

When Cunningham is in a dance, it tends to be "about" him; his presence evokes metaphor, story, association. By instinct, by position, and by the circumstance of his age, he plays a role. Here is neither a young dancer, pretending for the sake of a role to be young, nor an old dancer, pretending for the sake of the spotlight to be young. Cunningham has become his own subject—no matter what he does, the mere fact of his doing it is dramatic, his very presence a *memento mori*. Increasingly, as the years have passed, Cunningham has cast himself as odd man out. At least fifteen years ago, he began to set himself apart from the company, often taking the role of an on-stage director, genially scurrying about disposing his dancers.

Lately, he has been placing himself differently, furtively. Often the dancers seem to avoid, ignore, or suffer him. In *Gallopade* (1981), ostensibly a children's romp, he cannot keep up, and the dancers play games without him. The dance—one of several portrait-of-the-artist dances—can be read as the story of a dancing life, telling what it is like to dance and then not to dance, and showing what Cunningham's dances will look like without him.

There are five dancers in *Quartet* (1982), and Cunningham is clearly the one uncounted. This work finds its parallels in the many ballets in which a figure representing death comes between two lovers, but here Cunningham is separated from his partner by a figure representing youth. In the spring 1991 season at City Center, it was David Kulick (a very handsome young dancer) who separated him from Helen Barrow (a great beauty who is the company's senior female). When Cunningham stands between Kulick and Barrow and waves his arms in protest, your heart breaks for him. He is on stage with four dancers, but he is alone.

Cunningham uses the age-youth contrast to different effect in *Pictures* (1984), a series of frozen, floodlit groupings, with dramatic lighting that tends to obscure its lovely transitions. Cunningham enters the scene upstage, part way through the dance, but he lets us know that he stands at its figurative center. At the end, he stands alone on stage with Patricia Lent (in 1984 his newest dancer), holding her in his arms, so that they suggest a Pietà. Will she die, the image asks, grow old and stop dancing (here the same thing as dying), leave him (like Carolyn Brown, Sandra Neels, Viola Farber, Valda Setterfield, Karole Armitage, Meg Harper, and all the others)? Will she leave him, and will he carry on? After you've seen *Pictures* a few times, the whole dance builds towards the final moment.

More and more these days, this is what Cunningham's dances seem to be about: means of support; community. In a sense, it is what they have always been about. Just as, in a sense, all great dance works take dance itself as their subject matter,[10] Cunningham takes his company as his subject matter in all of what he always does. If ever there was a performance that said, "I can't go on, I'll go on," this was it.

Notes

1. Panel discussion moderated by David Vaughan as part of "Merce Cunningham and the New Dance," presented by the State University of New York's Programs in the Arts, 1987.
2. Unless otherwise noted, all Cunningham quotations are from an interview published as "The I Ching and Me" in *Dance Magazine* in March 1988. This particular quotation comes from an article published in *The Daily Texan* on February 14, 1977.
3. Through December 1984, all dates are from David Vaughan's chronological list of Merce Cunningham's choreographies published at the end of *The Dancer and the Dance, Merce Cunningham in Conversation with Jacqueline Lesschaeve*. New York and London: Marion Boyars, 1985.
4. Cunningham's investigative use of contemporary technologies—including the computer (which breaks information down into "bytes") and film and video shooting and editing techniques and devices—is a logical extension of his concerns with aleatory procedures, fragmentation, multiplicitous points of view, and erasure.
5. William Anastasi, personal communication.
6. Lesschaeve, *op. cit.*, 83
7. *Ibid.*, 119.
8. For example, in the article "The I Ching and Me," *op. cit.*
9. Carroll, Noël, and Sally Banes, "Cunningham and Duchamp," *Ballet Review* XI/2 (Summer 1983).
10. This idea was discussed by dance critic Arlene Croce in a conversation about *Le Sacre du Printemps* following the Joffrey Ballet's revival of the ballet broadcast on WNYC-FM's afternoon program called "Around New York."
11. Lesschaeve, *op. cit.*, 114.
12. The connections between Cunningham's work (and the Cunningham-Cage philosophy) and contemporary physics are many, and apparent even to the lay reader. For recent relevant articles on "chaotic systems" see *Science News* 139 (1991): 60, 70, 148, 182, 248; 140 (1991): 59, 200, 229, 239, 282.

Gymnasium Event #1, Queensborough Community College, 3 April 1968. Photo © James Klosty, courtesy Cunningham Dance Foundation.

Walkaround Time, 1968. L to r: Carolyn Brown, Valda Setterfield, Meg Harper, Gus Solomons jr, Merce Cunningham. Photo by Oscar Bailey, courtesy Cunningham Dance Foundation.

Canfield, 1969. Photo © James Klosty, courtesy Cunningham Dance Foundation.

Sounddance, 1975. L to r: Ellen Cornfield, Chris Komar, Karole Armitage, Louise Burns, Rob Remley, Merce Cunningham.
Photo © 1992 Johan Elbers.

Squaregame, 1976. Karole Armitage and Merce Cunningham. Photo by Charles Atlas, courtesy Cunningham Dance Foundation.

Travelogue, 18 January 1977, premier performance at the Minskoff Theater, New York. Photo © Jack Vartoogian.

Tango, 1978. Photo by Nathaniel Tileston, courtesy Cunningham Dance Foundation.

Galopede, 1982. L to r: Merce Cunningham, Rob Remley, Judy Lazaroff, Robert Swinston. Photo © 1992 Johan Elbers.

Phrases, 1985. Merce Cunningham and Catherine Kerr. Photo © Tom Brazil.

Points in Space, 1986. L to r: Chris Komar, Robert Swinston, Karen Radford. Photo by Robert Hill for the BBC, courtesy Cunningham Dance Foundation.

Roaratorio, 1986. L to r: Megan Walker, Alan Good, Catherine Kerr, Merce Cunningham, Rob Remley, Dennis O'Connor, Kristy Santimyer. Photo © Tom Brazil.

Fabrications, 1987. L to r: Alan Good, Chris Komar, Merce Cunningham. Photo © Jack Vartoogian.

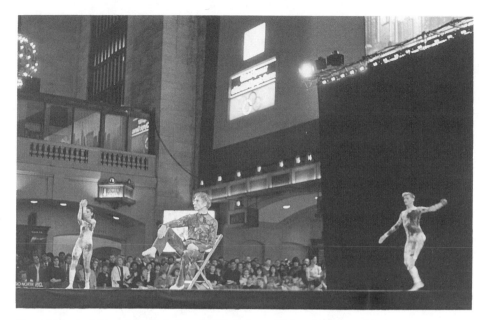

Grand Central Event, 9 October 1987. L to r: Helen Barrow, Merce Cunningham, Dennis O'Connor. Photo © Tom Brazil.

Merce Cunningham, John Cage, and company, 1988. L to r: Victoria Finlayson, Catherine Kerr, Dennis O'Connor, Alan Good, Megan Walker, Patricia Lent. Photo © Jack Mitchell.

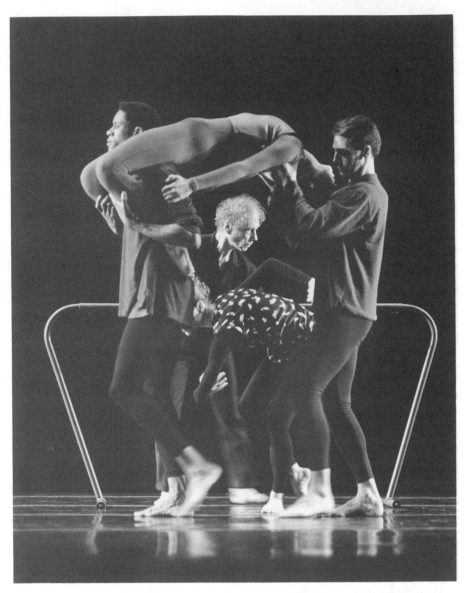

Trackers, 1991. L to r: Michael Cole, Merce Cunningham, Carol Teitelbaum, Robert Wood, Emily Navar (in the air). Photo © 1992 Johan Elbers.

Kenneth King

SPACE DANCE AND THE GALACTIC MATRIX: MERCE CUNNINGHAM, AN APPRECIATION (1991)

Merce Cunningham is our first Space Dancer. His galaxy of dances has expanded the parameters and horizons of modern dance, heralding the post-modern. Our conceptions of space, its boundaries and reality, and his radical ideas about time and structuration (through his lifelong collaboration with John Cage) have challenged the givens of our perception, and our presuppositions about the art of the dance.

Merce is the Einstein of modern dance. More than anyone, he has found **mind** in dance. Merce dances the **idea**; his **systems dances** are kinetically animated treatises (videotexts, now, too!) that are cognitive and hyperdimensional. In fact, Merce Cunningham has been the singular most revolutionary (i.e. transformative) modern artist (and the most advanced choreographer on the planet) whose dance combines, extends, and breaks the codes of both modern dance and ballet. So after nearly twenty-five years of watching his work—a great pleasure—one feels prompted by the impossible to sketch an Appreciation.

Merce Cunningham is a man who obviously likes to muse on many things at once; his dancing, and the diversity of his large repertoire, roams and *ranges* over immense distances and galactic terrains. His own dancing is always characterized by a certain, ineffable, fleeting touch, his fingers are always probing and slightly vibrating, then reaching, letting the whole body sluice its

187

way deliciously through space with an elfin musicality. An uncanny, visceral awareness permeates the registers of his physicality; his head is sensor and antenna—a bristling punctuation underscores all the ways his movement pulses create dynamic surprises, unusual placements, and wonderfully unexpected linkages. Legs and lines strike in sharp, clear distinction, both severing and opening space, moment, mind. Here, too, to appreciate his dances, we need the words of Gaston Bachelard: "... *they must be lived in their poetic immensity.*"[1]

Merce's body was the first to **systemically** synthesize ballet and modern dance to find all the multiplex ways the contracting and rotating spine could work with and against the mechanics of the legs to create planar shifts and **axial** transformations, and the first to register the **digital pulse,** coincidentally, around 1950, at the time when TVs were entering every household. (The digital pulse links *three* contracting spinal and thoracic zones in the lower, middle, and upper spine. And: when you pulse, contract, **and** rotate the spine's "*geomimetric*" facings, you get the metatheoremics of robotics! Merce's dance is already a kind of futuristic Artificial Intelligence with a concrete, cogent reflexivity of kinetic possibilities. So there!) It was the **digital pulse** that enabled him to transform the frequencies of his choreography, and extend the synchronicity of multiple temporal modalities.

Merce is **pure** semiotics—before they became an international intellectual practice and enterprise! Codes, signals, and signs provide the **multi**lectic of Merce's **modus kinecti!** Merce Cunningham's dances realize William James's prophetic projection of contemporary words and ideas like **digital, field, event, import** (instead of meaning as literality), and kinetic pluralism—cornerstones of essential Cunningham which take on new meanings, and—treatises. (James was working with these ideas *before* Einstein, and **before** the 1890 publication of *The Principles of Psychology.* Imagine William James watching Merce and company! His scientific eye, pragmatic sensibility, and seminal modernism would be delightfully challenged.) Merce realized the digital *kinetrics* of structural relativities; actually, **schematologies** of relativities which underlie the structurations of his dances, the animation of a stage **continuum,** and the hyperdimensionality of the body through extended, high-frequency, spatial ambients. (His dances *also* generate vectorially circuited biospheres, motoric continuums, and kinetic (e)ideograms.)

I first saw Merce Cunningham and Dance Company in *Variations V,* a multimedia extravaganza-spectacle at Lincoln Center in 1965, with music by John Cage and David Tudor (the floor had been miked to incorporate the sound made by the dancers' feet as a compositional component) and multimedia by Stan VanDerBeek (film) and Nam June Paik (TV images). During the latter part of the sixties and early seventies, I saw several of Cunningham's seasons at the Brooklyn Academy of Music which featured such works as *Antic Meet* (1958), *Nocturnes* (1956), *Winterbranch* (1964), *Crises* (1960; a revival, with

Viola Farber), *Summerspace* (1958), *Canfield* (1969), *Signals* (1970), *Scramble* (1967), *Walkaround Time* (1968), *TV Rerun* (1972), *Objects* (1970), *RainForest* (1968), *Tread* (1970), *Place* (1966), *Second Hand* (1970), *Borst Park* (1972), and *Landrover* (1972), among others.

By this time, Merce's work had already sparked a controversy of misappropriated critical response. Critics—surprised or bewildered by the shift to unconventionally formal, discontinuously lyrical priorities, and the patent lack of emotive, romantic, literary, or psychological supports—called his work "non-referential." How could an avant-garde dancer be a non-referential lyricist?!

What Merce Cunningham actually discovered of course was **how** movement of whatever mode or register can create its *own contexts* and, further, how those contexts can flexibly shift the focus, perspective(s), and dimensionalities within the internal logi(isti)cs and cohesiveness of a dance. (The **form** of a dance depends on the accountability of its **structures**.)

The critics' "non-referential" disclaimer sabotaged recognizing the wider esthetic and structural processes of composition, the registers of abstraction, the expanded conceptual permutations of form, and their semiotic transformations. (We've had descriptive journalistic criticism instead of dance literature; Merce, though, is worthy of a Paul Valéry, Maurice Merleau-Ponty, or a Jacques Derrida.) I have always been interested in the reflexivity of his dances and movement invention (their *modus operandi*)—how they kinetically mirror the rigorous principles of their deployment, and their uncanny intellection that makes them scrupulously fascinating. In terms of spatial plasticity, sculpture is probably the closest art to dance, with and without analogies. Merce *sculpts* space by attending to the multiplex details of each individual figure in the rapid continuum transformations within the ongoing intricacies of his ensemble.

Merce Cunningham has scored still *another* first, which is probably already taken for granted—he's the first choreographer to forge, develop, and exemplify **synergetics** in the dancing body, creating "**geokinenometrics**" or *multilexical* structural architectonics. His repertory is a parallel galactic shorthand, whose comprehensive functionalities are (meta)theoretically mirrored and exposed in R. Buckminster Fuller's two-volume source primer, and *magnum opus, Synergetics,* a monumental superlogical systemicity of numerically ordered entries spanning technological, engineering, and mathematical disciplines, somewhat recollecting the unique logistical, typological ordering of Wittgenstein's *Tractatus Logico-Philosophicus*, but whose seminal interdisciplinary typographizing comes **after** technology, electronics, and atom smashing. The transactions between processes and system are the techno(onto)logical horizon of the arts and sciences. That a multiplicity of rhythmicized structures can create interactive continuums, that dance steps can **synergize** to raise the frequency of the dancing body, and that a heightened body frequency can process several streams of *digitation*—information—and cognition **is** *Merce's* invention.

The origin of both the synergetics of the movement, and the structural fusion of modern dance and ballet, undoubtedly have their roots in the formative development of his early work, around 1952, that began at Black Mountain College (the celebrated experimental school that initiated an entire modern-art movement, where John Cage staged the first "happening"), where Merce met Bucky, and where both initially collaborated. Two of Merce's first, most dedicated, and special dancers, Carolyn Brown and Viola Farber, brought a unique set of complementary talents and originary contrasts that synergized the combined stylistics of those two predominant dance forms. The balletic polarity can be traced to the immaculate artistry of Carolyn Brown; her pristine classical precision, and the beautiful, lyrical ideality of her placement and being, heightened the modernist impulse. Viola Farber, on the other hand, was quixotically quirkier—like silly putty with surefire hyperplex instincts, and with an angular, wiry, and sinuously off-centered flexibility. Merce, of course, magically merged both sets of qualities in his own dancing and in the later development of his company.

Cunningham's field-continuums **("Events")** developed in the late 1960s as a free-wielding, more flexible (and economic) repertory format, synchronistically recombining sections of dances, collaging excerpts and activities, thus merging disparate materials while also permuting new structural variables (also creating omnitopologies [Fuller's word]), paralleling the "open systems" of microbiologists. Though the structuralities of his dances are always clearly delineated, delimited, and pluralistic, ply and play with multiple modes (and codes) of patterning and configuration, their form always remains open, and open to further horizons of possibilities. (Of course Merce's dances all coordinate synchronistic factors and structures, **but** within the cohesion of a specific work; Events span and interconnect the broad range of *all* his works.) In fact, Merce Cunningham's dances are virtual and systemic *treatises*—he's gone the furthest in carrying abstraction of form, its temporal and spatializing processes and presentations, to new, all-inclusive thresholds.

How movement is form, filament, and function of **space** is Merce's unique praxis and insight. In her great three-volume book, *Mind: An Essay on Human Feeling*, Susanne K. Langer says: "The problems of abstraction in art have never been philosophically surveyed and analyzed."[2] Just as John Cage's sonic experiments might be said to explore physiognomic hearing (and neuroacoustics), Merce's dancing celebrates a kinesthetically active physiognomic seeing. (Also: a *kinelexically* active seeing, or the way we *read* different, simultaneous kinetic orders of movement, motion, and animation.) His calibrated choreographies might well exemplify Edmund Husserl's conceptual term—**kinemathics**—the mathematical components of (con)figurated kinetics, or, **kinetrics**—as (meta)*systems* of topologically transactive kinetic possibilities.

Over the years, part of the reflective pleasure of watching Cunningham's dances has been trying to puzzle out their "genealogies"—their seeming "family resemblances"—how they relate to, reflex with, grow out of, or from, previous works, or share an adjacency with them, but it is always in a new vein, not just additively. Right away, one differentiates the serious from the humorous pieces. *Antic Meet, Borst Park, Roadrunners* (1979), and *Grange Eve* (1986), with its whimsical, offbeat vaudevillian trappings, are hilarious, absurdist spoofs—dance farces.

The serious dances in turn are of two basic kinds: either systems-oriented, like *Canfield, Torse* (1976), *Landrover*, and *Fractions* (1977), or dramatic dances, such as *Winterbranch, Quartet* (1982) *RainForest*, and *Points in Space* (1986). (*Winterbranch* is a stark apocalyptic work; *Canfield*, based supposedly, at least in title, on a kind of solitaire, was an early, perhaps the first, evening-length **systems dance** with a mysterious floating light sculpture/decor by Robert Morris that slowly transversed the foreground of the stage casting an imposing, stark shadow along the backdrop during its elongated passage. *Canfield* might well have been the turning-point between repertory and the development of Events. *Canfield* was a muted, somber, **existential** dance whose extended *duration* seemed to forge a new programmatic continuum. Perhaps that dance stylistically shares a "family resemblance" with highly rigorous, dramatically portending works like *Exchange* [1978]. Two other full-length works that preceded *Canfield* and *Landrover* were *Variations V* and *Walkaround Time*.)

Signals dates back to 1970, made before *Landrover*, but I believe both occurred around the same time that the systems choreography we now associate as staple Cunningham was inaugurated. *Signals* is episodic; it begins with an intriguing trio of two men and a woman. One man maneuvers a magic wand or long stick to energize and define the sharp spaces between their bodies. There are specific sections: solos, trios, duets, etc., and at various times during its performance, non-active dancers sit on a few folding chairs placed in an upstage corner.

Landrover is much more spatial; it spans a huge, implicit expanse. It is one work that cogently clarifies the dialectic of bodies and space, geometry and geography. The ground of one's body geometry is anchored by the vertical axis of the spine, which can reposition the use of one's weight and balance, and the ways vectors and lines are coordinated from the dancer's visceral center, creating (omni)directionality, and the complex, vertiginous contours of projected, virtual space. "Geography" refers to the spatial implementation of patterns in typographizing space, and their patterned extendabilities.

In a conversation in his studio, when asked about *Landrover*, Merce Cunningham said that the idea occurred to him because of all the company's travels; he wondered how a dance might appear if the background, or scenery, were always changing. (A landrover, of course, is a kind of caravan vehicle. In

(We know James championed a no-nonsense, concrete, everyday lexicality, but some fancy literary equipment is necessary too; Merce is our cosmic ornithologist, plotting complex flights with fleet feet. So, when watching a Cunningham performance, I often imagine William James in his **own** private balcony box delightfully bewildered, puzzled, and thrilled about what he sees, testing and inquiring as to just **what** can be said: how movement reflexes [a phenomenological] intentionality, how codes inform the dances' underlying structural permutabilities, the compositional complexities of a movement field, the dynamics of the discontinuous, especially with regard to aligning divergent **processes,** and synergizing systematic elements and rhythms, the margins of indeterminism [and the "margins" of movement and visibility: eidos and gestalt], digital geomimetrics, multidimensionality, would be some of the esthetic issues and "problems" that surely would fascinate him.)*

Of course it is well-known that Merce Cunningham utilizes chance operations to overcome the personalisms of decision-making, following John Cage's practice. Very simply put, chance is an objectifying means to remove motives and egos from dance making, and is the means to break the given, temporal logic or structure of a phrase, and the expectations of movement's order and sequence. Chance too covers many methods of composition, and enables Merce to play with the blind spot of the eye, the visual tricks that accrue as the eye sweeps and scans the performance and space of any given dance, and the cognitive manifold that switches between perception and apperception, processing and entraining the bundles of after-images. (Its logistics still baffle experts and audiences alike.) The point is that **intentional** structures (Husserl, again) superseded "motivated," psychological, and emotive movement, and prepared the field so that discrete and fragmented dance materials could discontinuously **but** formalistically collage space and bodies, thus moving all their (implicit) kinetic imageries and registers past their usual frames of reference, generating a palpable plurality of meanings, or polysemia.

Synchronicity and chance create an unusual spontaneity in the performance of the entire repertory, which can also be deceiving; some viewers are fooled into thinking that the dances are improvised, and one might say that Merce is so adept that he can **simulate** the look of an improvised spontaneity, but, of course, the simulacrum he's tapped into is the synchronicity of multiple *digital* rhythms. (This simulacrum points in the direction of dancers' true freedom and artistic autonomy, by giving the **semblance** of navigating through space on their own

---

*Several words need careful, topical clarification: **eidetic, mimetic,** and **kinetic.** The eidetic (from the Greek word *eidos*) refers to the clarity of prehending the visual, virtual, mental contours and factorealities of phenomena. The mimetic originated with language (and art), and refers to the animation of the elemental factors and action(s) of the processes underlying (linguistic) perception, and, with regard to dance, suggests all the ways signals and signs (con)figure in the perceptual field. Kinetics refers to motion and movement factorealities; kinetrics to the system(at)ic interfaces of movements and structures. Kinesthesia is a separate sense matrix, the total sensibility that apprehends all the orders of motion perception. *Kinelexia* refers to the modes and codes of how movement gradients and a dance's intraleveraged structural plays are "read."

decisions.) Synchronicity involves the parallel and/or concurrent synchroniza-tion of diverse rhythms, melodic, and motific elements; the results of the (intra)coordinated cycles and unexpected linkages of steps and structures are always surprising. Maybe even more than being the master structuralist, Merce is the multiplex *structurations* expert, since the decentralization of the spatial focus recircuits the given, hierarchical conditioning of our organized perceptual habits. In Merce's dances, synchronicity makes for **systemicity,** the concatena-tion of pluralistic, multiplex details and overlapping visual scanning reflexes deployed through formal contexts and their implicitly resonating, virtualized registers. *Systemicity,* as the axial interconnectedness of movement systems, makes Merce one of the first true choreographers!

A constant dialectical interplay between an individual dancer and the interpression of ensemble configurations informs the orchestration of each work. A quick, ready analogy for structural transformations, rules, and trans-positions of choreographic operations is computer games, which depend on the constant **digitality** of recomposable configurations. It's the p(l)ace(s) be-tween patterns, pathways, and passages that locate(s) the pluriverse's plural-istic diversity, and the cosmic intervallics, of his compositions.

Instead of stories, **placements** make **relations** between bodies, and steps register, cohere, and have import; instead of psychology, a dancing calculus; instead of motivation, **intentionality;** instead of an ego, a field. And though the essential key is structurality, Merce's dances always exemplify dramatic ideas, as in *RainForest* where he seems to be a paternalistic, or strong authorita-tive figure in the midst of a charged and restless drama, or perhaps a general or leader in *Exchange* (1978), and a totemic guardian, spirit, or near invisible ancestor in *Quartet* (1982). Instead of adumbrating actual locations, Merce's dances seem to inhabit and celebrate **scapes;** *Rebus* (1975), for example, seems to occur in a classroom as the matrix or ground for the variety of the dancers' work routines—but in a **dream** classroom with surrealistic dislocations and lyrical relocations of space, that continually recontext the dancers' festive contestings. The viewers' "problem" is apperceiving the riddle of the dance's patterns, rhythms, pulses, and structural juxtapositions; the axial axio-mat(h)ics of the rotating spine and configurative logics, and the planar concen-tration of pulses, reveal the daily ritualizing processes, different dancerly endeavors, and company interactions. (There's a modern metal clothes rack in the upper left stage corner covered with appropriately concealing garments that Merce periodically disappears behind, changes, and reemerges from, and in one sequence—his "dakini" solo—he is hidden behind a clover clump of four dancers who splay and fall to the floor revealing Merce in a svelte red unitard, very whimsically and dramatically plying tiny, quizzically meticulous details and gestic changes!) *Rebus* is a dance of red sensuality, with richly textured, sharp, and quixotically punctuated dynamics and hyperspatialized **qualities**, which the steps serve to generate and heighten.

planar spirals and paramechanic insignia, onto transparent plastic cubes of varying sizes that the dancers moved behind and around. The choreography discontinuously combined activities with informally overlapping episodes; it was also balletically leggy and elongated, and cut through space punctuated with sharp falls, structural foils, and stillpoints—moments and figures frozen in the shifting panoply of sections and activities. (Even the intermission was a programmatic part of the dance, in which the dancers, in rehearsal attire, or dressed in slippers and protective clothing, went through their usually unseen offstage rituals.) This dance thus accentuated and intensified the perception of multiply contexted, diagrammatic zones and cubistic planes in space—human beings interacting with space and structures, and **space** itself . . . empty, but an entity nonetheless.

The space around the dance(s) is also important, sometimes, as important as the dance, since it sets off its virtuality and presentational foci. Works like *Squaregame* (1976) point this up by removing all the backdrops and side-stage curtains, revealing a naked backstage area with pipes and ropes, and by using a pristine white floor cloth to accentuate the dance's centered spatial placement. The dancers, in sporty pastel garments (by Mark Lancaster), periodically pass, toss, lounge by (and, in Merce's case, humorously hides behind) duck white canvas gym bags (the large kind used in football scrimmage), while moving through complex, athletically bounding ensemble subgroupings that mix and merge. The energy and excitement of the work are additionally punctuated by the extra margins of space that further set off the totality of all its interlacing rhythms and mimetic details.

This kind of extended and suspended placement of the dance moved all the way toward a *galactic* realization when the company performed a week of Events at the 66th Street Armory on Park Avenue in New York City in June 1983. The spectacularly vaulted spatial expanse, as large as a city block and several stories high, architechtonically advanced the space-age dimensions and volumetrics of Merce Cunningham's work. The "off-stage" margins of the performance space (in full view) were active, dynamic ingredients in seeing and recycling the virtual **tao**tality (and the perceiver's scan patterns) of his work, letting us see how the dancers exit and make off-stage transitions. (The margins of the performance space are akin to the peripheral field of vision where, according to Marshall McLuhan, we *field* new information.)

There's an anecdote in John Cage's book *Silence* about Merce and space— as if his studio were analogous to the confines of a backyard, a bound and limited space, but one that opens onto the unbound if every inch is carefully utilized—a marvelous metaphor for the tending and expansion of space. In *The Poetics of Space*, Gaston Bachelard considers how (the creation of) a site can both condense quanta of detail, then open out on immensity. The esthetics of expansion and contraction of space and the dialectics of qualities, contrasts of scale, and the tensities that support it, are topics that Susanne K. Langer treats in "A Chapter on Abstraction" in the first volume of *Mind: An Essay on Human Feeling*.

*   *   *   *

One of the most magical moments I've ever witnessed in Cunningham's work is the solo finale to *Place* (1966), which I saw at the Brooklyn Academy of Music. A dramatic, existential dance with a patch-like constructivist rear-wall set made out of a white, lattice-like grid with attached, corrugated designs (and highly contrasted, zone-shifting lighting) by Beverly Emmons, this dramatic group dance created quite some controversy. It generated rumors that Merce was "alienated" from the company; he became a decentralized solo figure, very much in the back, making lone, mysterious moves, suggestive gestures, and aloof connections whenever he entered or passed through the dance, sometimes creating an unusual contrast by his presence or placement, sometimes instigating or dispersing relationships, other times gently touching a group of dancers, tapping them on the shoulder with a benign shrug as if to say "enough"—as if paternity or authority could be dispensed with.

At the very end of the dance, on an empty stage, he came all the way downstage alone, suddenly holding a sack, which was done so quickly the viewer had no idea where it had come from, and somehow, again without seeing how, he managed to climb into it—the lights were already beginning to fade and all this happened very rapidly—as he rolled on the floor upstage toward darkness and the void, the sack just up to his chest, his eyes beady and urgent, his sense of imminent disappearance interrupted by the falling curtain. Surely this is a moment Samuel Beckett would have cherished—archly existential, also profoundly and magically mysterious.

*   *   *   *

Torse was both a systematic **and** *systemic* breakthrough. Systematic because the carefully calculated progressions of the repetition variations of the steps and sections of the dance were mathematically plotted and spatialized. (In interviews, Merce explained that he used the ancient Chinese book of wisdom, the *I Ching*, with its sixty-four hexagrams, to map out the work's spatiality, to organize the dance's internal structure, and to typographize the ensemble sections.) *Systemic* because the repetition variations further heightened the accreting and fractionating mimetic "integers" and dynamic "coefficients" of the seriated steps and structures, their plastic transformations and themic permutations. The staggered temporal modalities recombined (often in one's afterimagings while watching, or remembering), then concatenated, both in the branchings of their transassociative eidetic suggestions, and in terms of their actual **quantum** impact on perception. The continually transformative structurations options, codes, borders, and parameters of Merce's dance are analogous to differential equations that charter the way systems continually change, permute, and transmute, not without reference (and relevance, too) to the linguists' "deep grammar," transformational rules, and mirror itself is the instrument of a universal magic that changes things into a spectacle, spectacles into things, myself into another and another into myself . . ."[3]

* * * *

If *Torse* and *Fractions* are advanced field theory, then *Sounddance* is **quantum mechanics!** Though it's impossible and ludicrous to even attempt to have a "favorite" Cunningham dance, *Sounddance* still seems to be in, and have, a category all its own. Choreographed in 1975, the program quotes a concisely ironic Joycean citation: "In the buggunning is the woid, and in the muddle the sounddance" (also cited in Norman O. Brown's *Closing Time*). *Sounddance* was made during the period of Merce's *very* high energy space dances; **very** stretched, driven, and electric!

The curtain rises on an empty stage. Mark Lancaster designed the white costumes, decor, and lighting. Upstage, a bare pipe used for hanging scenery has been lowered halfway and remains in full view; from it is suspended a kind of white canvas material slit in the middle, as an opening. The set reminded me of a (cosmic) magician's cabinet, or possibly a **solar** tabernacle. David Tudor composed an absolutely magnificent, intergalactic score, *Toneburst*, whose powerful acoustic volumetrics amplified the electrochromatic profiles of chordal strings, sounding like cosmically magnified celery fibers being stripped, and their overtone clusters split apart—like popcorn!—heavy crackling and galactic sounding interference creating immense reverberations, sonic blasts, and (implicit) stellar spaces. (David Tudor is due special credit; his amazing, powerful compositions are more space-age and futurological than the other composers, and his music perfectly synchronizes acoustic volumetrics with the kinetic amplitudes and precise sculptural architechtonics of Merce's dances.)

In the beginning, Merce is propelled out of the cleft in the fabric; the momentum, and its bristling, charged dynamic, suggest that he has been thrust into *this* space from an unknown source, realm, or dimension. From the very beginning of the dance until the very end a **tremendous** vibration is palpable. (It's a genuine gooseflesh experience!)

The dancers enter one at a time, but almost horrifically because the energy is so mighty it's all they can do to manage. They skitter, tilt, lurch, careen. Perhaps Meg Harper or Ellen Cornfield enters first, the other(s) shortly afterwards. Then, after the full company has assembled, bodies bolt to the floor, bound back, then are buffeted, thrown, tossed; they're rhythmically jittery and spastic, but always **dynamimetically** fluid. (Rhythm and dynamic have their own elusive musicological counterpoints and differentials; rhythm refers of course to all the metered, metrical, and cadential portionments of musical time; dynamic is more elusive—a kind of **tonus** that modulates and is modulated by the temporal unitizing of rhythms.)

Toward the beginning, Merce grabs the hand of one dancer—as if to rescue and steady her quivering impulsiveness—as her feet bleat, knead, and strike rapidly against the floor. The movements were not only extremely fast, dexterously flexed, and articulate, but their vectors slice across all seeming directions liberating untold stores of energy. The dance was sinuous, non-stop, and elastic—bouncing, hopping, and *popping*, too—it **exploded! This dance was from another universe!** Its design suggested both an archaic as well as futuristic dimension. The group choreography fluidically linked tensegrity structuralities so that vectors (equi)calibrated and supported unusually tensile body volleys at high kinetic momentum whose interface included split-second, acrobatic finesse: dancers lifted, carried, swept, and tossed. The dance seemed to split apart the movement matrices that held it together, and the impulses that figurated (and fragmented) the intricate phrases, and their dynamics played with atomizing the rhythmicity of the passages of the movement, perhaps, by analogy, the way James Joyce put morphemics and syntax into his holy atomic cyclotron in *Finnegans Wake*.

Sounddance reminded me of the restless tremors of an acid trip—a certain abrasive, **t-h-r-o-w-n** dynamic, and sprung propulsion **vigorously** hyperanimated each dancer. As they converged, a manic edge, thrilling and apocalyptic, scattered the impulses of their movements in bounding waves that surged and swept fluidly and propulsively across the stage. *Sounddance* broke open the codes of movement, spilling the complex dynamic ingredients and valences, balletic and modern—even the codes of Merce's oeuvre, too. This dance could also be seen as a celebration of electricity, cosmic electricity . . . or solar fire. Movement **can** release the energy of the cellular, genetic, and phonemic.

At the climax, Merce performed an absolutely amazing series of rapid, high-frequency, covertly suggestive hieratic gestures, his legs in parallel position, his torso smoothly spiralling and rotating with great forceful pulses that fluently rippled across the body while arms, then hands, unfurled imprecating and magical gestures with a secret, liquid virtuosity, and supreme mythic amplitude, supreme gestures, **Mahamudras,** fingers in ecstatic release, causing currents and shudders. Though hyperanimated and magically manic, there was a bristling ecstasy too, the way Walt Whitman might celebrate the **body electric** if plugged *directly* into a lightbulb or turbine!

This dance also seemed to have both a cosmic and Buddhist reference. The cleft in the drop cloth suggested a cavernous, primordial source, cosmogonic metaphor, too—the void behind the origin of the world (also womb-like). One Buddhist tenet is that sound and vibration precede creation; sound thus is anterior to, and originates before, image and appearance. It suggests the way creation spins and sp(l)its out its individuated particulars. The dance's overriding dramatic edge was apocalyptic because of the intense, loud, highly condensed, physicalized acoustic energy. There was something anxious, urgent, and sonically shattering—here Merce **is** the wizard of the galactic matrix—perhaps, ideally, foreshadowing the futuric merger of the step with higher neurotropic processes that Susanne Langer adumbrates at the very end of the third volume of *Mind: An Essay on Human Feeling*. (Galactic space is neither inner nor outer, objective nor subjective, a paralogical shift has occurred). Like Nikola Tesla (to whom Merce dedicated *Canfield* in 1969), who was photographed at the World's Fair early in this century, sitting nonchalantly inside a huge, high-frequency dynamo in an electrically charged field rife with crackling bolts and flying sparks all around him, Merce inhabits **kinetically** accelerated electromagnetic realms. (When I first saw *Sounddance* I remember telling him that it is very definitely the *first* **intergalactic** dance; maybe it's from Jupiter! It realizes a higher frequency, futuristic and higher dimensional ambience, and reveals an exciting transcendental realm quite unlike any other ballet or dance I've ever witnessed.)

Sounddance might also take place in a wind tunnel, or in a twilight realm between worlds, or between the interstices of dimensions. Toward the end there is another palpable dynamic transformation, as the dancers are "pulled" singly backwards and out of the space, disappearing one by one into the slit in the rear canopy, and the momentum builds further until Merce is left alone, and, as the final ante builds, he's spun and pivoted upstage. Just as he is about to crash into the cleft, the stage curtain comes down leaving the audience drenched in vibration, before they're on their feet screaming! Maybe it was at the last performance of the work when I overhead a woman behind me say to her companion: "**That** was supernatural!"

*   *   *   *

These descriptions are not just the dances' meanings, nor only this writer's interpretations, but rather the explicit, denotative structures, the trails and tracers of images and imageries, that sweep across the resolution screen of one's watching dancing (a new epistemic). Merce is fond of saying in interviews that he begins a dance alone in a studio, by taking a step. He insists his business is just to make the movement, **but** movement *does* transmit imageries, reflexes the wor(l)d and our experience, suggesting correspondences and analogies. How or why there are images in the mind, or, sometimes several simultaneous streams of movement imagery in a dance, has been deemed complex and unknown (cf. Susanne K. Langer in *Philosophical Sketches*).

Merce's **systems dances** of the late sixties and seventies were complex works transformative of every artistic factor, including our perception, and whose import extends through realms other than dance too. Merce's dances and **dancing** *are* metaphysical, and he has written that dance is the natural double for metaphysical problems and paradoxes. Merce is a man who has danced **beyond** shadow and double. An **otherness** always informs the grain and gain of his work. (Merce has often expressed his admiration for Fred Astaire, notably on his Guggenheim application in 1951. Everything is meta-physical, one can claim. Though both are incomparable, in spite of all the high-scale, commercial production values in Astaire's movies, *Merce* is the more classical, metaphysical, contemplative, and intellectual innovator.)

For Merce, the galactic matrix means operating at ontothetic space scales equilibrating higher frequency phases of being. In Buckminster Fuller's words:

> But frequency, as a word key to a functional concept, never relates to the word one because frequency obviously involves some plurality of events . . .[4]
>
> The physical Universe is an aggregate of frequencies. . . . The different frequencies of one element's set produce unique cyclic-frequency interactions whose resonances are similar to musical chords . . . The human senses are able to tune in no more than one-millionth of the total known frequency range limits of the presently known electromagnetic spectrum.[5]

From Buckminster Fuller's far-ranging chapter, **Conceptuality** in *Synergetics* (Volume I):

> Frequency is plural unity. Frequency is multicyclic fractionation of unity. A minimum of two cycles is essential to frequency fractionation. Frequency means a discrete plurality of cycles within a given greater cyclic increment.[6]
>
> Science has not found any continuous surfaces, solids, straight lines, or infinitely extensible, nonclosed-system planes.[7]

Then: omnitopology, vector equilibrium, pattern integrities, all-space filling, axes of symmetry (and asymmetry), isotropic vector matrices, discontinuous compression have *concrete* parallel extensions in Merce's galaxy of dances:

> All of our vision operates as an omnidirectional TV set, and there is no way to escape it. . . . But all vision actually operates inside the brain in organic, neuron-transistored TV sets. . . . All we do is deal in brain images.[8]

Merce's work inaugurated the modernist-dance focus on structure and system. The chapters in *Synergetics* on structure, system, and conceptuality in their entirety have a direct relevance, with far too many passages than can be cited here. For example:

> A structure is a self-stabilizing energy-event complex.[9]
>
> Constellar means an aggregation of enduring, cosmically isolated, locally co-occurring events dynamically maintaining their interpositioning.[10]
>
> It is a tendency for patterns either to repeat themselves locally or for their parts to separate out to join singly or severally with other patterns to form new constellations.[11]
>
> A system is a closed configuration of vectors. It is a pattern of forces constituting a geometrical integrity that returns upon itself in a plurality of directions. . . . Systems have an electable plurality of view-induced polarities.[12]
>
> Planet Earth is a system. You are a system.[13]

Systems can spin. There is at least one axis of rotation of any system.[14]

Systems can orbit. Systems can contract and expand. They can torque; they can turn inside out; and they can interprecess their parts.[15]

There is another great 20th-century philosopher who most certainly would have had a unique insight and appreciation of Merce Cunningham. That thinker, who shares a profound ontopoetic kinship with Paul Valéry and is the heir to the philosophical legacy of Henri Bergson, is Maurice Merleau-Ponty, whose on-tothetic analyses of the facticity of physicality and corporality advanced the phenomenological researches of the human body more than any of his predecessors. Merce in turn has forged an active phenomenology of the dancing body that cerebrates and **calibrates** the multiplistic interprecession of sights, signs, events, perspectivities, rhythms, and dimensionalities that reflexively mirror the cogent, (para)systemic dance of perception (i.e. the totality of a dance is more than its steps and structures). To quote Merleau-Ponty:

> . . . that body which is an intertwining of vision and movement . . . it is just as true that vision is attached to movement . . . the visible world and the world of my motor projects are each total parts of the same Being. . . . My movement is . . . the natural consequence and maturation of my vision. I say of a thing that it is moved; but my body moves itself, my movement deploys itself. . . . The enigma is that my body simultaneously sees and is seen . . . it sees itself seeing; it touches itself touching . . . the world is made of the same stuff as the body.[16]

Merce's dances celebrate the paradox of simplicity and complexity; any movement can be interesting, revealing, effective, if it is structured and rooted in a clear kinetic context—even if, or when, arrived at by chance. "Why worry about structure, it is always there," John Cage reminds us parenthetically in *Silence*.

The temporal invention of Merce's choreography is an intricate subject. *Not* dancing on the metrical beat, and not having his dances be dependent on music, were a watershed for Merce. Merce has proven that the autonomy of dance from music is a necessary liberty. In early interviews, John Cage, when discussing his studies with Arnold Schoenberg, explains why he had no interest in, and wanted to dispense with, harmony. Harmony, of course, supplies the flowing rhythmic coordinations of passages and movement, and figures differently as a compositional factor in dancemaking. Unlike Cage, Merce's dances are exemplary for their harmonics, meaning kinetically balanced tonics—of qualities, motor impulses, the flow of signs, rhythms, structural conjunctions, feelings, etc. Merce works with a synchronistic open form—graphs of structural possibilities—but, unlike Cage, whose scores involve improvised decision-making by the performers, once dice, or chance procedures, determine the sequences of a dance, the structure is set. (Supposedly the "fork in the road" was the celebrated 1963 UCLA performance that

Carolyn Brown has written about in Jim Klosty's photo and essay book, *Merce Cunningham,* that was one of the only, early occasions where the dancers could decide in performance variations to which the repertory could be subjected.) In composition workshops, and in his company, dancers have to be able to **know** how to kinetically measure time, which they learn by using stopwatches. But time can also be filled, measured, or used *without* being **metered**. Chance is another means to (ap)portion the temporal. Some works that celebrate multiplicity, like *Canfield, Landrover, Walkaround Time,* and *Torse,* involve an extended duration, and blur and suspend the accountability of a linear, sequence-specific response. Others seem to condense and encapsulate discrete and overlapping times, so that complex, synchronistic weaves of action, occurrence, and occasion play and ply a plurality of temporal **registers** (*Sounddance, Locale,* and *Changing Steps*).

Merce's biography *is* the landscape of his dances. (Someone has to write about Merce and John Cage and their biographical connections. Their long collaboration and the development of Merce's company provided Cage with an ongoing platform and laboratory; how the spectrum of his musical works and how his collaborations with Merce unite and diverge from his entire opus would make a very timely essay.) At the end of his solo, *Loops* (1971), which also concluded *Changing Steps,* Merce's lithe, supple hand gestures dramatically grab the air, twist, and feistily pull invisibles into his center, condensing and wrapping up the entire, formidable energy and **landscape** of the performance.

*   *   *   *

The dancer is **not** separate from the dance—motion is all-enveloping and transactional. Merce's dancers, always immaculately rehearsed, bring exemplary brio and style to the works they perform. The fact that the whole company is a collection of virtuosi (listed alphabetically) is taken for granted. So it seems natural in trying to recollect the specifics of a given dance to realize that the particular qualities are inseparable from what the dancers bring to their parts. In 1984, Merce choreographed *Doubles* for his lifetime-achievement award given by the Samuel Scripps Foundation at The American Dance Festival at Duke University in Durham, North Carolina. *Doubles,* a work for eight, was choreographed separately on two different groups of his company, to account for the structural variances and differences that each cast would bring to the work. Supposedly the parallel choreographies between the casts weren't rigid, and Merce worked with each separately, so steps *and* interpretations would vary. (This suggested the possible occasion for both groups to perform the work simultaneously, one behind the other, at a space site like New York's immense Park Avenue Armory on 66th Street.)

Merce's work is always new, always different, **always** challenging. And you have to puzzle it out—that's an invitation! I remember meeting the celebrated dance critic and poet Edwin Denby in 1983, after an Event, in the very back of the balcony at City Center in New York City, which we again agreed *is* the best location from which to watch dance (because **that's** where the eyes can **see** the *dynamic* image [Susanne Langer has clarified and differentiated the actual image from the dynamic image, which is the virtualized realization of all its projected qualities and elements.]). Upon attempting to recollect the totality of any given work, all the parts jangle in the mind's eye and in the reflex and challenge of (re)collecting them. I was surprised when Edwin, who had seen Merce's performances decades longer than I had, confessed that he, too, could not always identify the specific dances that are excerpted during an Event. Sections usually performed to a given score may be seen against another, in silence, and/or vice versa. This is always a puzzle, because the sections, dynamics, structures, and "takes" can be (or seem) easily recontexted.

*   *   *   *

In the summer of 1966, I studied with Merce at his studio, then on Sixth Avenue and 14th Street on the top floor of a building formerly used, shared (and found for him) by Julian and Judith Malina Beck of The Living Theater. During this time I learned his basic exercises, which I continue to do this day. Merce's technique is a kind of yoga that ingeniously combines modern dance and ballet in a new key.

The first surprise in technique class is the use of parallel legs, which ballet never uses, and that is actually quite difficult at first. This makes three physical feats, and demands, possible. First, it enables the dancers to work on their turnout, by pulling up from the inside of their thighs to connect and control the legs from the abdomen and high in the hips. Secondly, it enables the dancers to align the two (often nonsymmetrical) sides of their spine, which controls their whole body weight/axis from the top of the hips, and to isolate the segmented zones of the back so as to be able to drop their weight into the floor while **lifting** up their carriage and varying the back's modes of deportment. This gives dancers an extra spatial mobility to rapidly change tempi and direction. Thirdly, it secures the torso by isolating the hips to further enable a fluent series of segmented, isomorphic contractions and rotations of the spine so as to easily coordinate off-balance and decentered movement sequences.

Merce has always stood out from his company for his pliancy and plasticity of expression, his mimetic virtuosity, and his ability to transform expression into a new performative style. Merce is a great actor and comic, and in works like *Antic Meet*, *Borst Park*, *Roadrunners*, and *Grange Eve* the wizened vaudevillian emerges around the corners and edges.

In 1966, Merce gave one of his rare lectures at the 92nd Street Y (one of the mainstays of modern-dance concerts in the fifties and sixties). And though it was years before the popularization of video, there was a monitor in the lobby for latecomers enabling them to see Merce on stage in the process of his program. He began at a microphone with a modest but informative commentary, then turned on a tape recorder so his lecture could continue while he moved out onto the stage to perform solos that demonstrated some of the different structural and compositional problems he had set for himself. The dialectic of words and movement was tremendously insightful, revealing the careful methods and transformative processes Merce had discovered, and, in an indirect way, offered a performative solution to the bicameral mind-body linkage. Though the compositional factors always proceed from a formal concern, the dramatic contours, kinetic colors, and kinesthetic harmonics are always evident. Merce is clearly a man who *thinks* with his (whole) body.

* * * *

And, one shouldn't overlook the fact that the discovery and articulation of the dancing body in the late 20th century might not have proceeded without all the parallel, complex, and generative processes of language and language researches—linguistics, semantics, logical analysis, semiotics, structural and post-structuralism, etc. And though dance is a non-discursive art, learning it requires constant explanation for even the subtlest changes and qualities. The generation of sounds, words, memory icons, then phrases and syntax involves the constant concatenation and syntheses of neurotropic processes that constantly mix and merge the kinesiology of signals and signs in high interface, that are also the components of thinking. From William James's psychology, to Ernst Cassirer's study of symbolic forms, to Ludwig Wittgenstein's logical analyses, to Roland Barthes's awareness that language and the body are two of the (combined) fertile frontiers even as this century lurches toward completion, remind us that though dance is a non-discursive art, (formally) independent of semantic meaning, it **does reflect** the **tao**tality of experience. That dance is a language is already a moot point. Merce shies away from language and explanation, so it is easy to dismiss just how **axial** the interaction and parallel developments of language and dance **are.**

I've left the dance that initially had the biggest impact to last—*How to Pass, Kick, Fall and Run* (1965)—which dramatized the potency of a text for dance accompaniment. It was a fun piece, deceptively engaging, that collaged activities interseamed (it seemed) with a complex mixing principle at its center. John Cage began by popping a bottle of champagne that instantly caused the audience to rally to a convivial, party-like, celebratory atmosphere. The piece was accompanied by him reading a chance-ordered, musicologically metered medley of stories and anecdotes with purposeful, pregnant pauses, and which provided a bubbly and often ridiculous textual and **theatrical** counterpoint to the dance. But it was the syntactical, rhythmic, gestic, and kinetic **correlations** that lifted the dance out of the realm of the symbolic into a new domain of the concrete, giving new meanings to *meaning* as the **contexture** of a continuum—interprocessed processings threading activities and coincidences in wry, witty juxta- and superimpositions. The reverberations, articulations, and punctuations of the interlaced, cadential weaves between language and dance theatricalized the mercurial, often rapid shifts of contexts. Words build up other sonic-acoustic registers, references, and resonations, and are thus another (meta)musicological phenomena, providing a highly kinetic companionship. It's exactly what fascinates me to this day—two parallel and coconcurrent or **compossible** (Merleau-Ponty's word after Husserl) **processes** to bridge the brain's bicameral, hemitropic *dialexis,* to multiswitch its usually one-sided attunement(s).

Merce's dances are an emblematic reinforcement of futurity's presence; he is more than a choreographer of open spaces and galactic ranges; his high frequency works are also energy experiments that reveal new frontiers of frequency and registers of bioenergetic potential (realized) on a grand scale, ranking with such pioneers as Nikola Tesla and Wilhelm Reich. The **tao**tality of his work bridges East and West, activity and stillness. His work has taught us to **read** multiple kinelexic spectrums of movement. "Yes, truly we dream while reading,"[17] Gaston Bachelard reminds us, and we also dream while calmly and attentively watching dance (the mimetic having its source in the onieric).

*   *   *   *

Here are some brief, fragmentary recollections of memorable individual dancers' exceptional performances to help spark other organizational and mnemonic links.

I remember Carolyn Brown—fluid, mercurial, sleek, and fleet, always *tensile* too, in giving movement its due, its full body (not setting it up, as Merce sometimes does!) in *Winterbranch, Walkaround Time, Second Hand,* and *Tread* (the dance with huge industrial fans blowing full tilt on stage—*and* three more dances, too, to write about!).

I remember Viola Farber's languishing leggy hyperplex—purposely off-balanced stumbling, jangling, and gangling, with a wonderful hyperextendability—then punctuated by an arrested stillness; suddenly, astonishingly, one saw that space *too* has nerve(s)! In *Crises* (revived at the Brooklyn Academy of Music in 1969), she and Merce performed a duet connected at the hips by an enormous elastic band.

I remember Patricia Lent (1986) at the City Center Theater, and Catherine Kerr (1988) at the Joyce Theater performing the long, immaculate opening solo in *Doubles.* Patricia Lent often reminded me of Merce, the way she would lunge on the diagonal, her arms cleanly etching the surrounding air while inscribing arcs, punctuating her body moves through space with an exciting exactitude, and moving so that each point contrasted with every other point or body part; also her perfectly controlled, difficult, and sustained balances on one leg.

I remember Cathy Kerr in *Arcade* (1986) in what seemed to be a lead role (usually anathema for Merce) dancing with both detached, cool, yet fervent, intense finesse, like an Amazon or Egyptian priestess or regal statuary!

I remember Louise Burns, perky and quirky, and so resilient with refreshing athletic prowess in *Torse, Rebus, Duets,* and other works, busily brushing her feet, turning the tendu into an exotic item belying her thrill with a brisk attack and beaming smile.

I remember Chris Komar in *Torse* with Merce's mercurial, faun-like awareness amplifying his incredibly articulate performance of precise jumps, sharp, immaculate phrasing and delivery, at one moment reminding me of Thornton Wilder's *Our Town* in a wistful solo while the rest of the dancers were frozen in space with their backs to the audience (recalling Emily's death scene). I remember Alan Good and Megan Walker in the opening duet of *Coast Zone* (1983) in a kind of purely sculptural epiphany; their pristine partnering making the eye dart and swim in an effort to savor the *deliciousness* of their intricately shared, omnidirectional exchange.

I remember seeing at least eight performances of *Exchange* with severe, dark costumes and decor by Jasper Johns, and music by David Tudor, one of the most exciting and complex of all of Merce's dances; each viewing made me certain that either new sections had been added, or that it was impossible to perceive in its totality. It is a streamlined, subtly ritualized work that Merce created—like a kind of general, leader, or guardian; the work seemed to speak to the dark, uncertain dangers we are all facing, at times as if during a storm, with upheaval or war reverberating in the distance. (Thinking back on it now, it's a dance rich with duets and double exchanges, with a multiplicity of kinetic and dynamic logics and interactive, configuratively interpenetrating structures, though formal and abstract, actuating complex transformations, with many mysterious meanings and dimensions.)

I remember the company's opening night on Broadway (January 1977) when *Travelogue* was premiered with playful pastel silk drops and a mobile train of children's chairs and desks on a roll-on platform by Robert Rauschenberg pulled on at the beginning of the dance, and naturally, a terrific, poignant solo by Merce tilting with windmill arms and flexed feet, Chaplinesque. I remember Merce's careful hand-to-mouth silent scream in *Scramble,* a bright, modern, full-company work with pastel-colored screens on wheels by Frank Stella, that somewhat resembled, and that could be moved like, tennis accoutrements, which were rearranged for the various sections.

I remember *Roaratorio* kicking off the Next Wave Festival at the Brooklyn Academy of Music in 1987, Merce's spectacle of an Irish circus with a densely multilayered, wildly cacophonous score by John Cage that combined site-specific sounds, music, and bagpipes from Joyce's Dublin, with text weaves derived and transposed from *Finnegans Wake.* It was preceded by *Inlets 2* (1983), a gorgeous, truly **pure** dance that was totally complete and that could have been an evening-in-itself—very sculptural in the way it released the integrity, grain, and tones of motion, and their inhering sets of qualities. (Supposedly a "pure" dance is a contradiction of terms, possibly akin to the Buddhist "subject"—which doesn't exist!)

I remember the delightfully goofy finale to *Borst Park* performed on the stage of the Opera House of the Brooklyn Academy of Music, with the musicians featured on stage; at the end, the dancers attempt to serve a picnic; a red-checkered tablecloth is laid down, but quickly begins *moving* across the stage as the gregarious gaggle of dancers gambols and scrambles to follow it, *and* **as** a RUBBER CHICKEN is pulled out of a wicker picnic basket and tossed on it, while the curtain is falling (with the audience falling out of their seats laughing!).

I remember Merce downstage in his Westbeth New York studio (with a glorious aerial view of the sparkling nightlit megacity below) around 1980 very close to the audience in an Event performing an excerpt from *Landrover* with arms outstretched, flicking and rotating, making powerful, outwardly directed gestures and zapping me in the front line of focus. I remember Merce at the end of *Changing Steps* performing his *Loops* solo—reaching, grabbing, and pulling invisibles out of the air with a very uncanny, magical finesse. I remember the March 17, 1982 (to be precise) Event on a Thursday night at City Center that was also very magical—the stage suddenly became empty (after an excerpt from *Winterbranch*). There was a huge, unrecognizable door covering the entire rear wall; when it was unexpectedly thrown open it revealed a massive, cavernous backstage area, Merce was standing there alone. It sent a charge surging through the whole audience. I remember Merce's (animal) *Solo* that began with him upstage in profile walking *en passé* as if he were approaching the void (the left side of the stage being much darker) then turning, and, in the course of the dance, animals appeared—suddenly an iguana or lizard, serpentine and aquatic, as he snakily shifted his hips while the tongue flickered, then later on the floor making circular, preening-like feline hand (or paw) movements around his head like an endearingly furry mammal. I remember the last performance of *Sounddance* (at City Center) as the audience immediately rose, stood, stomped, applauded, hooted, cheered, bravo'd—whistling, screaming—**SHRIEKING!**

to be continued . . .

NOTE: Special Thanks to Marjorie Gamso, Anne Lall, Mary Lisa Burns, and Ted Marks for their editorial suggestions and corrections.

Notes

1. Gaston Bachelard, *The Poetics of Space* (Boston: Beacon Press, 1969), 210.
2. Susanne K. Langer, *Mind: An Essay on Human Feeling* (Baltimore, MD: The Johns Hopkins Press, 1967), I:153.
3. Maurice Merleau-Ponty, "Eye and Mind," in *The Primacy of Perception* (Evanston, IL: Northwestern University Press, 1964), 168.
4. R. Buckminster Fuller, *Synergetics* (New York: MacMillan, 1975), 153.
5. Ibid., 249.
6. Ibid., 250, entry 515.30.
7. Ibid., 614.

SPACE DANCE AND THE GALACTIC MATRIX (1991)   213

8. Ibid., 440, sections 801.21/22.
9. Ibid., 314, entry 600.02.
10. Ibid., entry 600.04.
11. Ibid., entry 601.01.
12. Ibid., 97, entry 400.09.
13. Ibid., 102, entry 400.47.
14. Ibid., entry 400.60.
15. Ibid., entry 400.61.
16. Merleau-Ponty, "Eye and Mind," 162–63.
17. Bachelard, *The Poetics of Space*, 162.

CHRONOLOGY OF WORKS BY MERCE CUNNINGHAM

As of July 1992

Compiled by David Vaughan

MCDC = Merce Cunningham [and] Dance Company
NYCB = New York City Ballet
ABT = American Ballet Theatre
GRCOP = Groupe de Recherche Chorégraphique de l'Opéra de Paris
All solos danced by Merce Cunningham unless otherwise stated

TITLE	MUSIC	DESIGN	DANCERS	PLACE/DATE OF FIRST PERFORMANCE
Seeds of Brightness (Choreographed with Jean Erdman)	Norman Lloyd	Charlotte Trowbridge	Merce Cunningham Jean Erdman	Bennington, VT; 1 Aug 1942
Credo in Us (Choreographed with Jean Erdman)	John Cage	Charlotte Trowbridge	Merce Cunningham Jean Erdman	Bennington, VT; 1 Aug 1942
Renaissance Testimonials	Maxwell Powers	Charlotte Trowbridge	Solo	Bennington, VT; 1 Aug 1942
Ad Lib (Choreographed with Jean Erdman)	Gregory Tucker (John Cage 1943)	Charlotte Trowbridge	Merce Cunningham Jean Erdman	Bennington, VT; 1 Aug 1942
Totem Ancestor	John Cage	Charlotte Trowbridge	Solo	New York, NY; 20 Oct 1942
In the Name of the Holocaust	John Cage	Merce Cunningham	Solo	Chicago, IL; 14 Feb 1943
Shimmera	John Cage	Merce Cunningham	Solo	Chicago, IL; 14 Feb 1943
The Wind Remains (*Zarzuela* in one act after Federico Garcia Lorca)	Paul Bowles	Oliver Smith Kermit Love	Merce Cunningham Jean Erdman et al	New York, NY; 30 Mar 1943
Triple-Paced	John Cage	Merce Cunningham	Solo	New York, NY; 5 Apr 1944
Root of an Unfocus	John Cage	Merce Cunningham	Solo	New York, NY; 5 Apr 1944
Tossed as it is Untroubled	John Cage	Merce Cunningham	Solo	New York, NY; 5 Apr 1944

TITLE	MUSIC	DESIGN	DANCERS	PLACE/DATE OF FIRST PERFORMANCE
The Unavailable Memory Of	John Cage	Merce Cunningham	Solo	New York, NY; 5 Apr 1944
Spontaneous Earth	John Cage	Merce Cunningham	Solo	New York, NY; 5 Apr 1944
Four Walls (A Dance Play by Merce Cunningham)	John Cage	Arch Lauterer	Merce Cunningham Julie Harris et al	Steamboat Springs, CO; 22 Aug 1944
Idyllic Song	Erik Satie arr. John Cage	Merce Cunningham	Solo	Richmond, VA; 20 Nov 1944
Mysterious Adventure	John Cage	after David Hare	Solo	New York, NY; 9 Jan 1945
Experiences	John Cage Livingston Gearhart	Merce Cunningham	Solo	New York, NY; 9 Jan 1945
The Encounter	John Cage	Merce Cunningham	Solo	New York, NY; 12 May 1946
Invocation to Vahakn	Alan Hovhaness	Merce Cunningham	Solo	New York, NY; 12 May 1946
Fast Blues	Baby Dodds	Merce Cunningham	Solo	New York, NY; 12 May 1946
The Princess Zondilda and Her Entourage	Alexei Haieff	Merce Cunningham	Merce Cunningham Virginia Bosler Katherine Litz	New York, NY; 12 May 1946
The Seasons	John Cage	Isamu Noguchi	1 Ballet Society with Merce Cunningham 2 NYCB	New York, NY; 18 May 1947
The Open Road	Lou Harrison	Merce Cunningham	Solo	New York, NY; 14 Jan 1949
Dromenon	John Cage	Sonja Sekula Merce Cunningham	Merce Cunningham and group	New York, NY; 14 Dec 1947
Dream	John Cage	Merce Cunningham	Solo	Columbia, MO; 8 May 1948

TITLE	MUSIC	DESIGN	DANCERS	PLACE/DATE OF FIRST PERFORMANCE
The Ruse of Medusa (a lyric comedy by Erik Satie, translated by M. C. Richards, directed by Arthur Penn)	Erik Satie	Willem and Elaine de Kooning; Mary Outten	Merce Cunningham et al	Black Mountain, NC; 14 Aug 1948
A Diversion (also given in quartet and solo versions)	John Cage	Mary Outten; Merce Cunningham	Merce Cunningham; Sara Hamill; Louise Lippold	Black Mountain, NC; 20 Aug 1948
Orestes	John Cage	Merce Cunningham	Solo	Black Mountain, NC; 20 Aug 1948
The Monkey Dances (from *The Ruse of Medusa*)	Erik Satie	Mary Outten; Richard Lippold; Merce Cunningham	Solo	Black Mountain, NC; 20 Aug 1948
Effusions avant l'heure (later called Games; Trio)	John Cage		Merce Cunningham; Tanaquil LeClerq; Betty Nichols	Paris, France; summer 1949
Amores	John Cage		Tanaquil LeClerq; Merce Cunningham	Paris, France; summer 1949
Duet			Betty Nichols; Milorad Miskovitch	Paris, France; summer 1949
Two Step	Erik Satie	Merce Cunningham	Solo	New York, NY; 18 Dec 1949
Pool of Darkness	Ben Weber	Merce Cunningham	Merce Cunningham; Dorothy Berea; Mili Churchill; Anneliese Widman	New York, NY; 15 Jan 1950
Before Dawn		Merce Cunningham	Solo	New York, NY; 15 Jan 1950

TITLE	MUSIC	DESIGN	DANCERS	PLACE/DATE OF FIRST PERFORMANCE
Waltz	Erik Satie		1 Student group 2 Solo	Baton Rouge, LA; 27 June 1950 New York, NY; 24 Nov 1950
Rag-Time Parade	Erik Satie		1 Student group 2 MCDC	Baton Rouge, LA; 27 June 1950 New York, NY; 24 Nov 1950
Waltz	Erik Satie		Solo	New York, NY; 24 Nov 1950
Sixteen Dances for Soloist and Company of Three	John Cage	Eleanor de Vito John Cage Remy Charlip Merce Cunningham	Merce Cunningham Dorothy Berea Mili Churchill Anneliese Widman	Millbrook, NY; 17 Jan 1951
Variation	Morton Feldman	Merce Cunningham	Solo	Seattle, WA; 12 Apr 1951
Boy Who Wanted to be a Bird			Solo	Martha's Vineyard, MA; Summer 1951
Suite of Six Short Dances	Recorder pieces arr. W. P. Jennerjahn		Solo	Black Mountain, NC; Spring 1952
Excerpts from *Symphonie pour un homme seul*	Pierre Schaeffer with Pierre Henry		1 Merce Cunningham & group 2 MCDC (under the title *Collage*)	Waltham, MA; 14 June 1952 Black Mountain, NC; 21 Aug 1953
Les Noces	Igor Stravinsky	Howard Bay	Merce Cunningham Natanya Neumann and group	Waltham, MA; 14 June 1952

TITLE	MUSIC	DESIGN	DANCERS	PLACE/DATE OF FIRST PERFORMANCE
Theatre Piece (arranged by John Cage, poetry by Charles Olson and M. C. Richards, film by Nicholas Cernovitch)	David Tudor	Robert Rauschenberg	Merce Cunningham	Black Mountain, NC; Summer 1952
Suite by Chance	Christian Wolff	Remy Charlip	MCDC	Urbana, IL; 24 Mar 1953
Solo Suite in Space and Time	John Cage	Merce Cunningham	Solo	Baton Rouge, LA; 23 June 1953
Demonstration Piece			Student group	Baton Rouge, LA; 23 June 1953
Epilogue	Erik Satie		Student group	Baton Rouge, LA; 23 June 1953
Banjo	Louis Moreau Gottschalk	Remy Charlip	MCDC	Black Mountain, NC; 21 Aug 1953
Dime a Dance	19th century piano music selected by David Tudor	Remy Charlip	MCDC	Black Mountain, NC; 22 Aug 1953
Septet	Erik Satie	Remy Charlip	1 MCDC	Black Mountain, NC; 22 Aug 1953
			2 Rambert Dance Co	Glasgow, Scotland; 20 Nov 1987
			3 Pacific Northwest Ballet	Seattle, WA; 15 Nov 1989
			4 Repertory Dance Theatre	Salt Lake City, UT; 9 March 1991
Untitled Solo	Christian Wolff	Merce Cunningham	Solo	Black Mountain, NC; 22 Aug 1953

TITLE	MUSIC	DESIGN	DANCERS	PLACE/DATE OF FIRST PERFORMANCE
Fragments	Pierre Boulez	Remy Charlip	MCDC	New York, NY; 30 Dec 1953
Minutiae	John Cage	Robert Rauschenberg Remy Charlip	MCDC	Brooklyn, NY; 8 Dec 1954
Springweather and People	Earle Brown	Remy Charlip (Robert Rauschenberg, 1957)	MCDC	Annandale-on-Hudson, NY; 24 May 1955
Galaxy	Earle Brown	Remy Charlip	MCDC	South Bend, IN; 18 May 1956
Lavish Escapade	Christian Wolff	Merce Cunningham	Solo	South Bend, IN; 18 May 1956
Suite for Five in Space and Time (later called Suite for Five)	John Cage	Robert Rauschenberg	MCDC	South Bend, IN; 18 May 1956
Nocturnes	Erik Satie	Robert Rauschenberg	MCDC	Lee, MA; 11 July 1956
Labyrinthian Dances	Josef Matthias Hauer	Robert Rauschenberg	MCDC	Brooklyn, NY; 30 Nov 1957
Changeling	Christian Wolff	Robert Rauschenberg	Solo	Brooklyn, NY; 30 Nov 1957
Picnic Polka	Louis Moreau Gottschalk	Remy Charlip	MCDC	Brooklyn, NY; 30 Nov 1957
Collage III	Pierre Schaeffer with Pierre Henry		Solo	Pittsburgh, PA; 21 May 1958
Antic Meet	John Cage	Robert Rauschenberg	MCDC	New London, CT; 14 Aug 1958

TITLE	MUSIC	DESIGN	DANCERS	PLACE/DATE OF FIRST PERFORMANCE
Summerspace	Morton Feldman	Robert Rauschenberg	1 MCDC	New London, CT; 17 Aug 1958
			2 NYCB	New York, NY; 14 April 1966
			3 Cullbergbaletten	Stockholm, Sweden; 5 Oct 1967
			4 Boston Ballet	Boston, MA; 7 Nov 1974
			5 Théâtre du Silence	La Rochelle, France; 29 Oct 1976
Night Wandering	Bo Nilsson	Nicholas Cernovitch (Robert Rauschenberg 1963)	1 Merce Cunningham Carolyn Brown	Stockholm, Sweden; 5 Oct 1958
			2 5 by 2 Plus	Anchorage, AL; 3 Sept 1977
From the Poems of White Stone	Chou Wen-Chung poems by Chiang Kuei	Robert Rauschenberg	MCDC	Urbana, IL; 14 Mar 1959
Gambit for Dancers and Orchestra	Ben Johnston	Robert Rauschenberg	MCDC	Urbana, IL; 14 Mar 1959
Rune	Christian Wolff	Robert Rauschenberg (Mark Lancaster, 1982)	MCDC	New London, CT; 14 Aug 1959
Theatre Piece	John Cage		Merce Cunningham Carolyn Brown	New York, NY; 7 Mar 1960
Crises	Conlon Nancarrow	Robert Rauschenberg	MCDC	New London, CT; 19 Aug 1960
Hands Birds	Earle Brown	Robert Rauschenberg	Carolyn Brown	Venice, Italy; 24 Sept 1960
Waka	Toshi Ichiyanagi	Robert Rauschenberg	Carolyn Brown	Venice, Italy; 24 Sept 1960
Music Walk with Dancers	John Cage	Robert Rauschenberg	Merce Cunningham Carolyn Brown	Venice, Italy; 24 Sept 1960

TITLE	MUSIC	DESIGN	DANCERS	PLACE/DATE OF FIRST PERFORMANCE
Suite de Danses a work for television, directed by John Mercure	Serge Garrant	Jasper Johns	MCDC	CBC-TV, Montreal, Canada; 9 July 1961
Aeon	John Cage	Robert Rauschenberg	MCDC	Montreal, Canada; 5 Aug 1961
Field Dances	John Cage	Robert Rauschenberg (Remy Charlip, 1967)	MCDC	Los Angeles, CA; 17 July 1963
Story	Toshi Ichiyanagi	Robert Rauschenberg	MCDC	Los Angeles, CA; 24 July 1963
Open Session	Merce Cunningham	Merce Cunningham	Solo	Hartford, CT; 19 Mar 1964
Paired	John Cage	Robert Rauschenberg	Merce Cunningham Viola Farber	Hartford, CT; 21 Mar 1964
Winterbranch	La Monte Young	Robert Rauschenberg	1 MCDC 2 Boston Ballet	Hartford, CT; 21 Mar 1964 Boston, MA; 7 Nov 1974
Cross Currents	Conlon Nancarrow arr. John Cage (John Cage, Oct 1964)	Merce Cunningham	1 MCDC 2 US Terpsichore 3 Werkcentrum Dans	London, UK; 31 July 1964 New York, NY; 3 Oct 1980 Rotterdam, The Netherlands; 19 Sept 1984
Variations V	John Cage	Film: Stan VanDerBeek TV images: Nam June Paik	MCDC	New York, NY; 23 July 1965
How to Pass, Kick, Fall and Run	John Cage		MCDC	Chicago, IL; 24 Nov 1965
Place	Gordon Mumma	Beverly Emmons	MCDC	Saint-Paul de Vence, France; 6 Aug 1966
Scramble	Toshi Ichiyanagi	Frank Stella	MCDC	Chicago, IL; 25 July 1967

TITLE	MUSIC	DESIGN	DANCERS	PLACE/DATE OF FIRST PERFORMANCE
RainForest	David Tudor	Andy Warhol	MCDC	Buffalo, NY; 9 Mar 1968
Walkaround Time	David Behrman	after Marcel Duchamp	MCDC	Buffalo, NY; 10 Mar 1968
Assemblage a film for television directed by Richard Moore	John Cage David Tudor Gordon Mumma		MCDC	KQED-TV, San Francisco, CA; Oct–Nov 1968
Canfield	Pauline Oliveros	Robert Morris	MCDC	Rochester, NY; 4 Mar 1969
Tread	Christian Wolff	Bruce Nauman	MCDC	Brooklyn, NY; 5 Jan 1970
Second Hand	John Cage	Jasper Johns	MCDC	Brooklyn, NY; 8 Jan 1970
Signals	David Tudor Gordon Mumma John Cage	Richard Nelson Merce Cunningham	1 MCDC 2 Ohio Ballet	Paris, France; 5 June 1970 Akron, OH; 20 Feb 1981
Objects	Alvin Lucier	Neil Jenney	MCDC	Brooklyn, NY; 10 Nov 1970
Loops	Gordon Mumma	Jasper Johns	Solo	New York, NY; 3 Dec 1971
Landrover	Jasper Johns Gordon Mumma David Tudor	Jasper Johns	MCDC	Brooklyn, NY; 1 Feb 1972
TV Rerun	Gordon Mumma	Jasper Johns	MCDC	Brooklyn, NY; 2 Feb 1972
Borst Park	Christian Wolff	The Company	MCDC	Brooklyn, NY; 8 Feb 1972
Un Jour ou deux	John Cage	Jasper Johns	Paris Opéra Ballet	Paris, France; 6 Nov 1973
Westbeth a work for video directed by Charles Atlas and Merce Cunningham	John Cage	Mark Lancaster	MCDC	New York, NY; fall 1974

TITLE	MUSIC	DESIGN	DANCERS	PLACE/DATE OF FIRST PERFORMANCE
Changing Steps	John Cage	Charles Atlas (Mark Lancaster, 1978)	1 MCDC 2 Théâtre du Silence 3 Purchase Dance Corps	Detroit, MI; 7 Mar 1975 Paris, France; 17 April 1979 Purchase, NY; 2 April 1987
Video version directed by Elliot Caplan and Merce Cunningham				October 1989
Rebus	David Behrman	Mark Lancaster	MCDC	Detroit, MI; 8 Mar 1975
Solo	John Cage	Sonja Sekula	Solo	Detroit, MI; 8 Mar 1975
Sounddance	David Tudor	Mark Lancaster	MCDC	Detroit, MI; 8 Mar 1975
Blue Studio: Five Segments videotape by Merce Cunningham and Charles Atlas			Solo	WNET, New York, NY; Oct 1975
Torse	Maryanne Amacher	Mark Lancaster	MCDC	Princeton, NJ; 15 Jan 1976
Squaregame	Takehisa Kosugi	Mark Lancaster	MCDC	Adelaide, Australia; 24 Mar 1976
Video version, *Squaregame Video*, directed by Charles Atlas			MCDC	New York, NY; 1976
Video Triangle part of *Event for Television*, directed by Merrill Brockway	David Tudor	Mark Lancaster	MCDC	WNET, New York, NY; Nov 1976
Travelogue	John Cage	Robert Rauschenberg	MCDC	New York, NY; 18 Jan 1977
Inlets	John Cage	Morris Graves	MCDC	Seattle, WA; 10 Sept 1977
Fractions videodance directed by Charles Atlas and Merce Cunningham	Jon Gibson	Mark Lancaster	MCDC stage version	New York, NY; Nov/Dec 1977 Boston, MA; 26 Feb 1978
Exercise Piece I			MCDC	New York, NY; 25 Mar 1978

TITLE	MUSIC	DESIGN	DANCERS	PLACE/DATE OF FIRST PERFORMANCE
Exercise Piece II	John Cage	Mark Lancaster	MCDC	Toronto, Ontario; 18 Aug 1978
Exchange	David Tudor	Jasper Johns	MCDC	New York, NY; 27 Sept 1978
Tango	John Cage	Mark Lancaster	Solo	New York, NY; 5 Oct 1978
Locale filmdance directed by Charles Atlas and Merce Cunningham	Takehisa Kosugi	Charles Atlas	MCDC stage version	New York, NY; Jan/Feb 1979 Paris, France; 9 Oct 1979
Roadrunners	Yasunao Tone	Mark Lancaster	MCDC	Durham, NC; 19 July 1979
Exercise Piece III	John Cage	Mark Lancaster	MCDC	New York, NY; 23 Feb 1980
Duets	John Cage	Mark Lancaster	1 MCDC 2 ABT	New York, NY; 26 Feb 1980 New York, NY; 18 May 1982
Fielding Sixes	John Cage	Monika Fulleman (William Anastasi, 1986) Mark Lancaster for Ballet Rambert	1 MCDC 2 Ballet Rambert	London, UK; 30 June 1980 Manchester, UK; 11 Feb 1983
Channels/Inserts filmdance directed by Charles Atlas and Merce Cunningham	David Tudor	Charles Atlas	MCDC stage version	New York, NY; Jan 1981 New York, NY; 24 Mar 1981
10's with Shoes	Martin Kalve	Mark Lancaster	MCDC	New York, NY; 17 Mar 1981
Gallopade	Takehisa Kosugi	Mark Lancaster	MCDC	London, UK; 10 June 1981
Trails	John Cage	Mark Lancaster	MCDC	New York, NY; 16 Mar 1982
Quartet	David Tudor	Mark Lancaster	MCDC	Paris, France; 27 Oct 1982

TITLE	MUSIC	DESIGN	DANCERS	PLACE/DATE OF FIRST PERFORMANCE
Coast Zone filmdance directed by Charles Atlas and Merce Cunningham	Larry Austin	Mark Lancaster Charles Atlas	MCDC stage version	New York, NY; Jan 1983 New York, NY; 18 Mar 1983
Inlets 2	John Cage	Mark Lancaster	1 MCDC 2 GRCOP 3 Concert Dance Co. of Boston 4 Sharir Dance Co. 5 Rotterdamse Dansgroep 6 Charleroi/Danses	1 Lille, France; 26 Oct 1983 2 Paris, France; 3 Dec 1983 3 Cambridge, MA; 13 Apr 1986 4 Austin, TX; 11 Mar 1988 5 Rotterdam, The Netherlands; 9 Feb 1991 6 Charleroi, Belgium; 13 Dec 1991
Roaratorio	John Cage	Mark Lancaster	MCDC	Lille, France; 26 Oct 1983
Pictures	David Behrman	Mark Lancaster	MCDC	New York, NY; 6 Mar 1984
Doubles	Takehisa Kosugi	Mark Lancaster	1 MCDC 2 Rambert Dance Co.	1 Durham, NC; 27 June 1984 2 Birmingham, UK; 30 Jan 1990
Phrases	David Tudor	William Anastasi Dove Bradshaw	MCDC	Angers, France; 7 Dec 1984
Deli Commedia videodance directed by Elliot Caplan	Pat Richter	Dove Bradshaw	Student group	New York, NY; Jan 1985
Native Green	John King	William Anastasi	MCDC	New York, NY; 12 Mar 1985
Arcade	John Cage	Dove Bradshaw	1 Pennsylvania Ballet 2 MCDC	1 Philadelphia, PA; 11 Sept 1985 2 Philadelphia, PA; 14 Nov 1985

TITLE	MUSIC	DESIGN	DANCERS	PLACE/DATE OF FIRST PERFORMANCE
Grange Eve	Takehisa Kosugi	William Anastasi	MCDC	New York, NY; 18 Mar 1986
Points in Space videodance directed by Elliot Caplan and Merce Cunningham	John Cage	William Anastasi	MCDC stage version 1 MCDC 2 Paris Opéra Ballet	London, UK; May 1986 New York, NY; 10 Mar 1987 Paris, France; 6 Jun 1990
Fabrications	Emanuel Dimas de Melo Pimenta	Dove Bradshaw	MCDC	Minneapolis, MN; 21 Feb 1987
Shards	David Tudor	William Anastasi	MCDC	New York, NY; 4 Mar 1987
Carousal	Takehisa Kosugi	Dove Bradshaw	MCDC	Lee, MA; 18 Aug 1987
Eleven	Robert Ashley	William Anastasi	MCDC	New York, NY; 9 Mar 1988
Five Stone	John Cage David Tudor	Mark Lancaster	MCDC	Berlin, Germany; 16 June 1988
Five Stone Wind	John Cage Takehisa Kosugi David Tudor	Mark Lancaster	MCDC	Avignon, France; 30 July 1988
Cargo X	Takehisa Kosugi	Dove Bradshaw	MCDC	Austin, TX; 27 Jan 1989
Field and Figures	Ivan Tcherepnin	Kristin Jones Andrew Ginzel	MCDC	Minneapolis, MN; 17 Feb 1989
August Pace	Michael Pugliese	Sergei Bugaev (Afrika)	1 MCDC 2 Paris Opéra Ballet (excerpts)	Berkeley, CA; 22 Sept 1989 Paris, France; 23 Oct 1990
Inventions	John Cage	Carl Kielblock	MCDC	Berkeley, CA; 23 Sept 1989
Polarity	David Tudor	Bill Anastasi Merce Cunningham Carl Kielblock	MCDC	New York, NY; 20 Mar 1990

TITLE	MUSIC	DESIGN	DANCERS	PLACE/DATE OF FIRST PERFORMANCE
Neighbors	Takehisa Kosugi	Mark Lancaster	MCDC	New York, NY; 13 Mar 1991
Trackers	Emanuel Dimas de Melo Pimenta	Dove Bradshaw	MCDC	New York, NY; 19 Mar 1991
Beach Birds	John Cage	Marsha Skinner	MCDC	Zurich, Switzerland; 20 June 1991
Film version, *Beach Birds for Camera*, directed by Elliot Caplan			MCDC	New York, NY; Dec 1991
Loosestrife	Michael Pugliese	Carl Kielblock	MCDC	Paris, France; 10 Sept 1991
Change of Address	Walter Zimmerman	Marsha Skinner	MCDC	Austin, TX; 31 Jan 1992
Touchbase	Michael Pugliese	Mark Lancaster	Rambert Dance Co.	London, UK; 20 June 1992

SELECT BIBLIOGRAPHY
OF CUNNINGHAM CRITICISM

Adam, Judy, ed. *Dancers on a Plane/Cage Cunningham Johns*. NY: Alfred A. Knopf, 1990.

Brown, Carolyn. "On Chance." *Ballet Review* II/2 (Summer 1968).

Carroll, Noël, and Sally Banes. "Cunningham and Duchamp." *Ballet Review* XI/2 (Summer 1983).

Cohen, Selma Jeanne. "Avant-Garde Choreography." In *The Dance Has Many Faces*, 3rd. ed., ed. Walter Sorell. Pennington, NJ: a cappella books, 1992.

———, ed. "Time to Walk in Space: Essays, Stories and Remarks." Contributions by Clive Barnes, Carolyn Brown, John Cage, Arlene Croce, Merce Cunningham, Edwin Denby, Jill Johnston, David Vaughan. *Dance Perspectives* 34 (Summer 1968).

Copeland, Roger. "The Politics of Perception." In *What Is Dance?*, ed. Roger Copeland and Marshall Cohen. NY: Oxford University Press, 1983.

Croce, Arlene. "Notes on a Natural Man." *The New Yorker* (7 February 1977).

———. "Crises." *The New Yorker* (3 April 1989).

Cunningham, Merce. "The Function of a Technique for Dance." In *The Dance Has Many Faces*, 1st. ed., ed. Walter Sorell. Cleveland: World Publishers, 1951.

———. *Changes: Notes on Choreography*, ed. Frances Starr. NY: Something Else Press, 1968.

———. "Choreography and the Dancer." In *The Creative Experience*, ed. Stanley Rosner and Lawrence E. Abt. NY: Grossman Publications, 1970.

————. "The Impermanent Art." In *Esthetics Contemporary*, ed. Richard Kostelanetz. Buffalo, NY: Prometheus, 1978, 1989.

————. "You Have to Love Dancing to Stick To It." In *The Vision of Modern Dance*, ed. Jean Morrison Brown. Princeton, NJ: Princeton Book Co., 1979.

Finkel, Anita. "Kristy's Red Hair." *The New Dance Review* (July/August 1989).

Fleming, Bruce. "Thoroughly Modernist Merce." *Washington Dance View* (Autumn 1989).

Goldner, Nancy. "Cunningham Diary." *Bennington Review* (Sept. 1978).

Greskovic, Robert. "Cunningham as Sculptor." *Ballet Review* XI/4 (Winter 1984).

Grossman, Peter Z. "Talking with Merce Cunningham about Video." *Dance Scope* XIII/2–3 (Winter–Spring 1979).

Gubernatis, Raphael de. *Cunningham*. Arles and Paris: Editions Bernard Coutaz, 1990.

Harris, Dale. "Merce Cunningham." In *Contemporary Dance*, ed. Anne Livet. NY: Abbeville, 1978.

Johnston, Jill. "Modern Dance." In *The New American Arts*, ed. Richard Kostelanetz. NY: Horizon, 1965.

————. "To Whom It May Concern." In *Marmalade Me*. NY: E. P. Dutton, 1971.

————. "Jigs, Japes, and Joyce." *Art in America* (January 1987).

Jowitt, Deborah. *The Dance in Mind*. Boston: David Godine, 1985.

————. "Illusion of Choice—Acceptance of Chance." In *Time and the Dancing Image*. NY: William Morrow, 1988.

Klosty, James, ed. *Merce Cunningham*. NY: Saturday Review Press, 1975 (reprint, NY: Limelight, 1987).

Kostelanetz, Richard. *The Theatre of Mixed Means*. NY: Dial, 1968.

————. "Modern Dance." In *Metamorphosis in the Arts*. Brooklyn, NY: Assembling, 1981.

————. "Dance." In *Conversations with Cage*. NY: Limelight, 1988.

————. "Cunningham/Cage." In *On Innovative Music(ian)s*. NY: Limelight, 1989.

————. "Merce Cunningham." In *On Innovative Art(ist)s*. Jefferson, NC: McFarland, 1992.

Lesschaeve, Jacqueline. *The Dancer and the Dance: Merce Cunningham in Conversation with Jacqueline Lesschaeve*. NY: Marion Boyars, 1985.

Lorber, Richard. "From Cimabue to Cunningham." *Millennium Film Journal* (Fall–Winter 1981/82).

Macaulay, Alastair. "On the Clouds." *The Dancing Times* (August 1985).

————. "Found in Space." *The Dancing Times* (September 1987).

————. "Happy Hooligan." *The New Yorker* (27 April 1992).

Mazo, Joseph. "Merce Cunningham: Multiple Choice." In *Prime Movers: The Makers of Modern Dance in America*. Princeton, NJ: Princeton Book Co., 1984.

McDonagh, Don. *The Rise and Fall and Rise of Modern Dance*. Rev. ed. Pennington, NJ: a cappella books, 1990.

Reynolds, Nancy. "Chance is a Nickname for Providence." *Dance Magazine* (July 1990).

Schöning, Klaus, ed. *Roaratorio*. Konigstein, Germany: Athenäum, 1985.

Siegel, Marcia B. "Summerspace and Winterbranch," "Septet." In *The Shapes of Change: Images of American Dance*. NY: Henry Holt, 1980.

———. "Repertory in Spite of Itself." *Hudson Review* (Summer 1985).

Snell, Michael (pseud.). "Cunningham and His Critics." *Ballet Review* III/6 (1971).

Tomkins, Calvin. *The Bride and the Bachelors: Five Masters of the Avant-Garde.* Rev. ed. NY: Viking Press, 1968.

Vaughan, David. *Diaghilev/Cunningham*. Hempstead, NY: Hofstra University, 1974.

———. "Ashton versus Cunningham?" *Dancing Times* (July–August 1979).

———. "Merce Cunningham: Origins and Influences." *Dance Theatre Journal* I/1 (Spring 1983).

———. "Cunningham, Cage and Joyce: 'This long awaited messiah of roaratorios.' " *Choreography & Dance* I/4 (1992).

CONTRIBUTORS NOTES

JACK ANDERSON (b. 1935) has authored eight books of poetry and seven of dance history and criticism. He is a dance critic for *The New York Times*, coeditor of *Dance Chronicle*, and New York correspondent for *The Dancing Times* of London. He has taught dance history and criticism around the world.

CAROLYN BROWN (b. 1927) was a founding member of the Merce Cunningham Dance Company, originating many roles during her tenure from 1952–1972. She is currently writing her memoirs.

EARLE BROWN (b. 1926) is an internationally acclaimed composer. Influenced by avant-garde artists of the fifties, Brown developed new notation and scoring methods, and originated "open form" compositions that allowed for individual improvisation.

JOHN CAGE (1912–1992) was a distinguished American avant-garde composer. Along with Merce Cunningham, whom he first met in 1938 when he was teaching at the Cornish School in Seattle where Cunningham was a student, he has championed radically alternate methods of composition. He has been the music director of the Cunningham company since its inception in 1953.

REMY CHARLIP (b. 1929) is a choreographer, dancer, theater and film director, painter, designer, teacher, playwright, songwriter, and author of over two dozen children's books. While a member of the Cunningham company, Charlip designed sets and costumes for several dances, as well as performing in them. He has performed worldwide as a soloist and leader of his International All-star Dance Company.

ARLENE CROCE was the founding editor of *Ballet Review* from 1965–1978, and has served as dance critic of *The New Yorker* since 1974. Her dance writings have been collected in *Afterimages* (1977), *Going to the Dance* (1982), and *Sight Lines* (1987).

MERCE CUNNINGHAM (b. 1919) is one of America's greatest dancer/choreographers. His work has influenced countless new artists and dancemakers.

NANCY DALVA is a senior editor at *Dance Magazine*.

DON DANIELS is presently an associate editor of *Ballet Review*.

EDWIN DENBY (1903–1983) was, in his time, commonly acknowledged to be the dean of American dance critics. His complete dance writings were collected in 1987 and published by Alfred A. Knopf; his *Complete Poems* was published in 1986.

DOUGLAS DUNN (b. 1942) performed with Merce Cunningham from 1969 to 1973. He was a founding member and performer with Grand Union in the seventies. He currently leads his own company, choreographs, and performs as a soloist.

VIOLA FARBER (b. 1931) danced with the Cunningham company from 1953 to 1965, returning temporarily in 1970. She currently teaches dance at Sarah Lawrence College.

BARBARA FROST graduated in 1948 from Vassar College, whose alumni office lost track of her in the mid-1980s.

JILL JOHNSTON was the dance critic at *The Village Voice* in the 1960s; some of these reviews were collected in *Marmalade Me* (1971). She is currently writing a multivolumed autobiography that includes *Mother Bound* (1983).

KENNETH KING is a dancer/choreographer and writer, and Artistic Director of Kenneth King & Dancers/Company. He has been called an inventor and philosopher because of the diversity of his "transmedia" experiments and interdisciplinary explorations that combine dance, voices/texts, music, and technology. His prose and poetry have appeared in many magazines and anthologies.

RICHARD KOSTELANETZ (b. 1940) has written and edited scores of books of and about contemporary literature and art, including *Conversing with Cage* (1988) and *On Innovative Music(ian)s* (1989). As a composer, he has received annual Standards Awards from ASCAP; as a media artist, he has received grants and residencies for his work in radio, video, holography, and film. His visual art has been exhibited around the world. He lives in New York City.

ALASTAIR MACAULAY reviews dance, music, and theater for *The Financial Times* of London. During the 1988–89 season and again in 1992, he was guest-critic at *The New Yorker*. He founded *Dance Theatre Journal* in 1983. A collection of his writings on Frederick Ashton appeared in 1988.

DON MCDONAGH (b. 1932) has authored several books on dance, including *Martha Graham* (1973), *The Complete Guide to Modern Dance* (1977), and *The Rise and Fall and Rise of Modern Dance* (1990). He is currently the managing editor of *Ballet Review*.

WILFRID MELLERS, some time professor of music at the University of York, England, has authored many books about classic and contemporary music.

FRANK O'HARA (1926–1966) was a distinguished American poet and art historian and critic, whose work has been widely published.

STEVE PAXTON (b. 1939) performed with the Cunningham company from 1961 to 1965. He was one of the founding members of the Judson Dance Theater in 1962. He has performed and taught contact improvisation internationally. Winner of numerous awards and grants, he is currently a contributing editor to *Contact Quarterly*.

VALDA SETTERFIELD danced in the Cunningham company from 1964 to 1974. She continues to perform with her husband, dancer/choreographer David Gordon.

SYBIL SHEARER (b. circa 1918) was a distinguished dancer with the Humphrey-Weidman company, before making her solo debut in New York in 1941. Since the mid-forties, she has danced, taught, and choreographed in Chicago. She is currently Chicago correspondent for *Ballet Review*.

MARCIA B. SIEGEL (b. 1932) has collected her fugitive dance reviews in four books: *At the Vanishing Point* (1972), *Watching the Dance Go By* (1977), *The Shapes of Change: Images of American Dance* (1979), and *The Tail of the Dragon* (1991). She is also the author of *Days on Earth* (1988), a biography of Doris Humphrey. Dance critic for *The Hudson Review*, she teaches in the Performance Studies Department at New York University.

MARIANNE PREGER SIMON is now a psychotherapist in private practice in Whately, MA. She danced in Cunningham's first company from 1952 to 1958, and was the first dance critic for *The Village Voice*.

STEPHEN SMOLIAR began publishing dance criticism while finishing his doctorate in Applied Mathematics at MIT in 1971. He has since been involved in artificial intelligence research with particular attention to the application of technology to music. He has also composed music for dance and currently is review editor for *Artificial Intelligence*.

GUS SOLOMONS JR (b. circa 1940) danced with Cunningham from 1965 to 1968. He now directs his own dance company, for which he choreographs and performs, in addition to writing on dance.

CALVIN TOMKINS is a staff writer at *The New Yorker*. His classic profile of Cunningham was reprinted in the revised edition of his book *The Bride and the Bachelors* (1968).

DAVID VAUGHAN (b. 1924), born in London, England, has lived in New York since 1950 and has been associated with the Merce Cunningham Dance Company in various capacities since the 1960s, presently as its archivist. He has written *Frederick Ashton and His Ballets* (1976).

JAMES WARING (1922–1975) was a noted American dancer, choreographer, and teacher. A student of Cunningham's, he ran his own company from 1949–1966, while also choreographing for other leading international dance companies.

INDEX

All works otherwise unattributed are by Merce Cunningham.

Other titles of interest

JOHN CAGE
An Anthology
Edited by Richard Kostelanetz
237 pp., 64 illus.
80435-2 $14.95

MUSIC BY PHILIP GLASS
Updated Edition
Philip Glass
Edited by Robert T. Jones
264 pp., 50 photos
80636-3 $13.95

THE PARIS DIARY & THE
NEW YORK DIARY, 1951–1961
Ned Rorem
New introd. by Richard Howard
Preface to *The Paris Diary* by
Robert Phelps
431 pp., 29 illus.
80838-2 $16.95

ALL HIS JAZZ
The Life and Death of
Bob Fosse
Martin Gottfried
512 pp., 30 illus.
80837-4 $16.95

ALVIN AILEY
A Life in Dance
Jennifer Dunning
496 pp., 27 illus.
80825-0 $16.95

DANCE TO THE PIPER &
PROMENADE HOME
Agnes De Mille
Preface by Cynthia Gregory
643 pp., 42 photos
80161-2 $17.95

A DICTIONARY OF
BALLET TERMS
Leo Kersley and Janet Sinclair
Drawings by Peter Revitt
112 pages, profusely illustrated
with line drawings
80094-2 $9.95

MARTHA GRAHAM
The Early Years
Edited by Merle Armitage
135 pp., 24 photos,
15 line drawings
80084-5 $12.95

NIJINSKY, PAVLOVA, DUNCAN
Three Lives in Dance
Edited by Paul Magriel
288 pp., 185 photos and illus.
80035-7 $15.95

TAP!
The Greatest Tap Dance Stars
and Their Stories, 1900-1955
Revised Edition
Rusty Frank
Foreword by Gregory Hines
342 pp., over 200 illus.
80635-5 $19.95

MOHOLY-NAGY
An Anthology
Edited by Richard Kostelanetz
238 pp., 88 illus.
80455-7 $15.95

ALL AMERICAN MUSIC
Composition in the Late
Twentieth Century
John Rockwell
New preface by the author
294 pp.
80750-5 $14.95

JAZZ DANCE
The Story of American
Vernacular Dance
Marshall and Jean Stearns
New fore- and afterwords
by Brenda Bufalino
506 pp., 32 photos
80553-7 $16.95

Available at your bookstore

OR ORDER DIRECTLY FROM

DA CAPO PRESS, INC.

1-800-321-0050